Wicked

VICTORIAN

BOSTON

For my mother, Marian Mallory Wilhelm

CONTENTS

INTRODUCTION

Victorian Boston—the phrase evokes images of stately brownstone homes on tree-lined streets, of monumental churches, libraries and universities, the shrines of faith and reason. It brings to mind elegant works of art—a twilit cityscape by Childe Hassam, a Henry James novel of manners and ideas—and brilliant discoveries that changed the world like Alexander Graham Bell's telephone. Then, as now, the vision of Boston as a center of culture, learning and morality was proudly promoted by the city's elite.

But not too far beneath the surface, Victorian Boston had a wicked side that was growing faster than the city itself. Boston had thousands of saloons, both licensed and unlicensed, paying little heed to laws regarding hours of operation and Sunday closing. Many of the city's groggeries ran backroom faro banks or poker games with little fear of police interruption. The lowest dives became headquarters for violent criminal gangs. Though illegal, sports betting became a million-dollar business. Throughout the city, saloons, hotels and theaters were little more than fronts for brothels, operating freely in locations well known to the police. Confidence men from New York viewed Boston as easy money and plied their trade not just in saloons but also at the docks, railroad stations, hotels and even the sidewalks of Beacon Hill. Boston Police would follow up complaints and intercede when the order was disturbed but did little to prevent vice in the city.

Most citizens of Boston remained unaffected by the city's underground culture of vice. Of course, they read the newspaper stories and frowned upon such bad goings-on, but on a day-to-day basis, anyone not actively

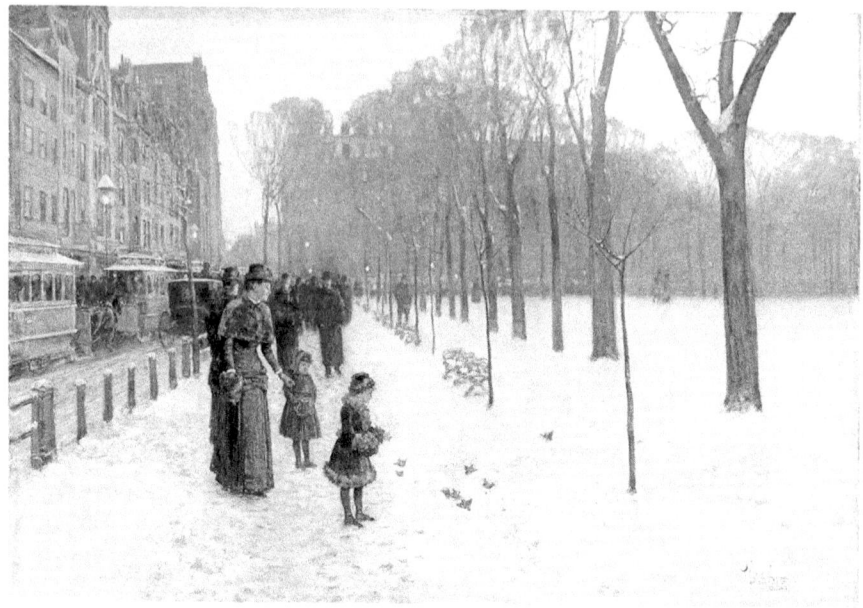

Boston Common at Twilight, Childe Hassam, 1885. *Wikimedia Commons.*

involved in immoral behavior could blissfully ignore it. But some found Boston's moral backsliding intolerable and believed that returning the city to its Puritan roots was essential to Boston's survival. As the city's population grew increasingly diverse, its cultural elite, consisting of prominent clergymen, educators and social reformers, moved to suppress anything that might further debase the lower classes or demoralize impressionable children—from saloons and brothels to indecent literature and immodest advertising. They called on Boston's patrician class to set an example and protect the innocent from corrupting influences.

But lines of morality were becoming blurred, and social standing was not a solid indicator of righteous behavior. The haunts of vice in Boston no longer catered exclusively to the common people; men of prominence frequented the lowest dives and brothels and even took ownership of them. Scandal rocked the finest families in Boston, as young debutantes dabbled in pornography, civic leaders were sued for domestic abuse and clergymen were charged with adultery. The seemingly endless string of very public court cases generated by Boston's disgraces drew the attention of the national press and added to the impression that the city was losing its moral compass.

The changing ethnic complexion of Boston in the Victorian era was also altering the nature of vice in the city. The rapid influx of Irish immigrants was disconcerting for the old Yankees; they despaired at the newcomers' fondness for hard drink and gambling and feared that the Catholic newcomers would owe their first allegiance to the pope of Rome. Xenophobia in Boston took the form of the anti-immigrant Know-Nothing Party, which briefly overwhelmed state and city politics.

But no one seemed to notice the miniature Chinese city growing in their midst. Chinese immigrants in Boston were happy to build their own society, with their own laws and customs, separate from the rest of the city. It would take a violent murder in 1886 to draw attention to Boston's Chinatown, revealing that the miniature city had an oversize network of vice, including prostitution, gambling and opium.

Victorian Boston was a battlefield in the war for the souls of men, with the forces of righteousness battling sin at every turn. Throughout the chapters of *Wicked Victorian Boston*, two names recur, their actions and words depicting the two sides of the moral war. On the side of darkness was Bose Cobb, an African American saloonkeeper whose dance hall was a center of depravity and temptation; and on the side of light was Reverend Henry Morgan, an outspoken Methodist minister who investigated Boston's vice firsthand and spoke and wrote in the most alarming terms of Boston's moral decline. These two men were the standard-bearers in the war that was won by neither side.

Unlike other American cities—most notably New York, Chicago and New Orleans—that seemed to revel in wickedness, making no attempt to

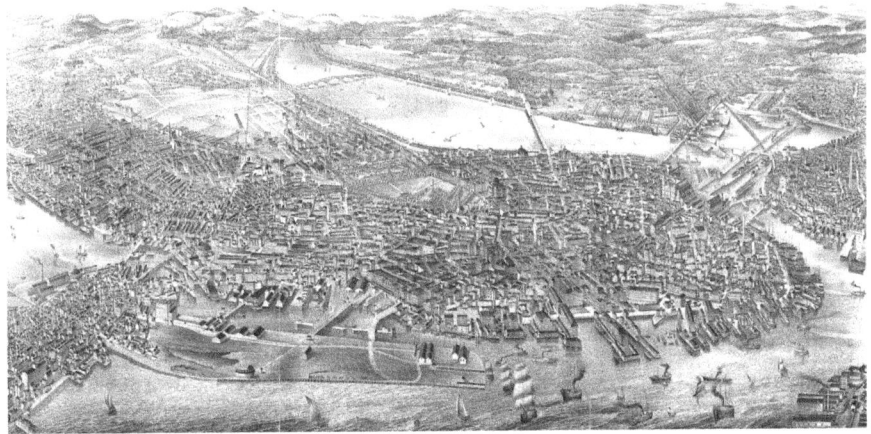

View of Boston, 1880. *Library of Congress.*

hide their vices, Boston preferred to sin in secret, speaking and writing of its transgressions reluctantly and then only to warn the unwary. Compiling a comprehensive history of vice in Victorian Boston would be a daunting task. This book, instead, is an anecdotal account of the characters and events that brought public attention to Boston's sinful side. The Victorian era was hardly the beginning of vice in Boston and its passing by no means meant its end, but for a brief time between the iron rule of Puritanism and the violence of twentieth-century organized crime, the city took some quiet joy in being wicked.

Chapter 1

SINS OF A GREAT CITY

Two men on a drunken spree in the early hours of August 8, 1885, decided to venture inside Bose Cobb's dance hall, drawn by the light and music pouring from its open door. James Barnes and George West entered the crowded barroom and were immediately approached by painted women looking for a dance and a drink afterward. West was willing, but amid the noise and chaos, Barnes realized he was drunker than he had thought. His partner found a bench where Barnes could lie down and sleep it off and then left him to join the fun. Some time later, Barnes awoke. Still drunk and now disoriented, he pulled a revolver from his pocket and brandished it in fear. West saw what Barnes was doing and rushed to his side, easily wresting the pistol from his hand, but Barnes had a second revolver, and this one went off, shooting West through the neck. James Barnes fled the scene before the authorities arrived to ask questions.

To a reader of dime novels, popular in the 1880s, a scene like this would feel familiar, evoking images of America's Wild West, but this event took place in the West End of Boston. Bose Cobb's dance hall on Norman Street was the most notorious of Boston's free-and-easies. Found in every major city at the time, free-and-easies were meeting places for sporting men, outlaws, slumming gentry and adventurous men of all classes. They were so called because of their free and easy approach to the law, particularly laws regarding liquor, gambling and prostitution, and for their egalitarian admission policy—at a free-and-easy, anything goes and everyone is welcome. Evenings in these resorts were often punctuated by violence, sometimes ending in bloodshed.

Some free-and-easies specialized in entertainment featuring musicians, dancers and comedians. Gray's Opera House in the West End was a saloon offering musical performances in direct violation of the city's liquor laws. In spite of its elegant name, Gray's Opera House did not stage operas. In fact, the quality of its entertainment was considered lower than that of a dime museum, but it launched the careers of several successful burlesque and variety performers.

Bose Cobb's place on Norman Street provided only enough music for dancing and had a ready supply of young women for men without partners. With its scofflaw approach to Boston's stringent liquor laws, its interracial dancing, two floors of illegal gambling, adjacent brothels and its frequent bloodshed, Cobb's was well known by sporting men across the country as one of the most infamous free-and-easies in America.

Of course, everyone in Boston knew of Bose Cobb's dance hall; his name in a news story meant vice and corruption, with no further explanation necessary. But the free-and-easies, the gambling "hells," the houses of ill fame were not the real Boston; they were the haunts of outsiders—transients, sailors on leave, emancipated slaves and the waves of immigrants arriving daily. To the average churchgoing citizen, Boston, at its core, was still the Puritan City.

Boston in the Victorian era was seen as the moral and intellectual capital of America. In 1858, Oliver Wendell Holmes referred to the Boston Statehouse as "the hub of the solar system," implying that Boston was the center of everything important. This epithet, later expanded to "The Hub of the Universe" and often shortened to just "The Hub," was, somewhat grudgingly, accepted by the rest of the nation. Boston was the "Athens of America," the "Puritan City," leading the fight for the abolition of slavery and for a free and, above all, moral society.

But among the city's righteous elite—clergymen and Boston Brahmins who felt a strong sense of responsibility for the moral behavior of others—there was a growing sentiment that vice in Boston had reached dangerous proportions. In 1885, Boston had two thousand licensed saloons, one for every 180 citizens, and perhaps one thousand more unlicensed. While not all were as wild as Bose Cobb's, even the quietest saloon could ruin a man's life or break up a family through drunkenness, and every saloon held the threat of gambling, prostitution and violence. And it wasn't just saloons; the fruits of laxity in public morals were everywhere. Theater galleries had become little more than bordellos, and their stages were filled with dancers in pink tights. Graphic public advertisements featuring

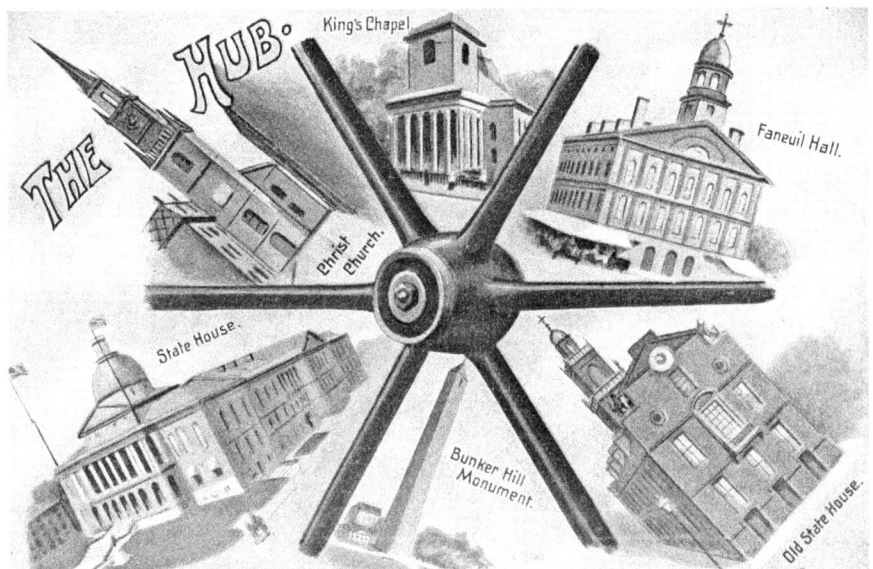

The Hub, postcard. *Author's collection.*

semi-clad actresses and newsstands selling publications with uncensored illustrations and stories glorifying crime and violence were displayed in plain sight of impressionable children. Scandals involving adultery and domestic violence were erupting among the city's better families. All this depravity would be expected in New York, the Sodom of America, but Boston was better. For the moral leaders, the city was on the road to hell, and something had to be done to turn it around.

They formed groups, each fighting vice in its own way—the Woman's Christian Temperance Union, the Law and Order League, the Young Men's Christian Association, the New England Society for the Suppression of Vice and so on. Many of those involved, actively and financially, were the same people who had fought for the abolition of slavery. When that sin was vanquished, the fight against vice seemed like the next logical step.

Individual crusaders joined the fight as well, and chief among them was a charismatic and provocative Methodist minister named Henry Morgan. Though he had a church of his own—the Morgan Chapel on Shawmut Avenue in the South End—it proved too small to hold the number of people anxious to hear him speak on the sins abounding in Boston. He periodically rented out the Boston Music Hall, with three thousand seats, and filled them all with ardent followers.

Reverend Morgan's message, resounding so loudly, was that Boston had lost its way by abandoning the values upon which it was founded. "Alas alas! The Boston of 1776 is no more! Puritanism has given way to modern paganism. Patriotism to greed. Devotion to sensuality. Sacrifice for self."

Morgan investigated Boston vice directly with the aid of a staff of agents, and he always came to his lectures armed with shocking statistics. In an 1878 lecture, he claimed he had discovered eight thousand prostitutes working in the city of Boston, a number that remained constant despite two thousand deaths in their ranks each year. He put the blame where it was due; the

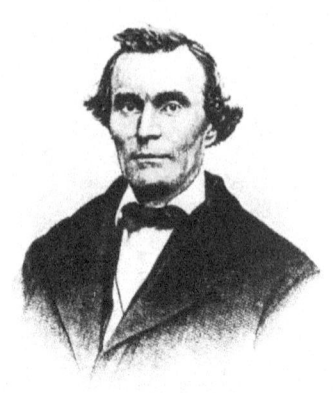

Reverend Henry Morgan. *From The Shadowy Hand, 1874.*

cause was "Men, lecherous men!" But as a self-styled Poor Man's Preacher, Morgan did not blame the poor workingman at home with his family. "The rich, idle spendthrifts are the city's curse. The law does not reach them. They go scot free."

Reverend Morgan visited all of Boston's "haunts of inequity"—dance halls, gambling "hells," spiritualistic mediums, quack doctors and saloons that opened on Sunday ("There are more persons in the groggeries of Boston on Sunday than in all the Protestant churches combined").

Morgan was a master at self-promotion and a tireless worker; when he wasn't lecturing on sin, he was writing about it. His novels—*Ned Nevins the Newsboy; or, Street Life in Boston*, published in 1867, and *Shadowy Hand; or Life-Struggles: A Story of Real Life*, published in 1874—depicted the rise of vice in Boston and prescribed a return to the gospel as a remedy. His bestselling book *Boston Inside Out! Sins of a Great City! A Story of Real Life*, published in 1880, generated six editions and sold at least twenty-five thousand copies. Writing *Boston Inside Out!* as fiction allowed Reverend Morgan to illustrate his message by contriving elaborate scenes and extreme characters—corrupt businessman Augustus Gildersleeve, lecherous priest Father Titus and innocent country girls Minnie Marston and Rose Delaney—leaving their true identities up to the reader.

In the book, Morgan explains how he had come to investigate vice in Boston. On a trip to Europe, Reverend Morgan is appalled by what he sees. The public immorality, gambling and drinking on the Sabbath, particularly

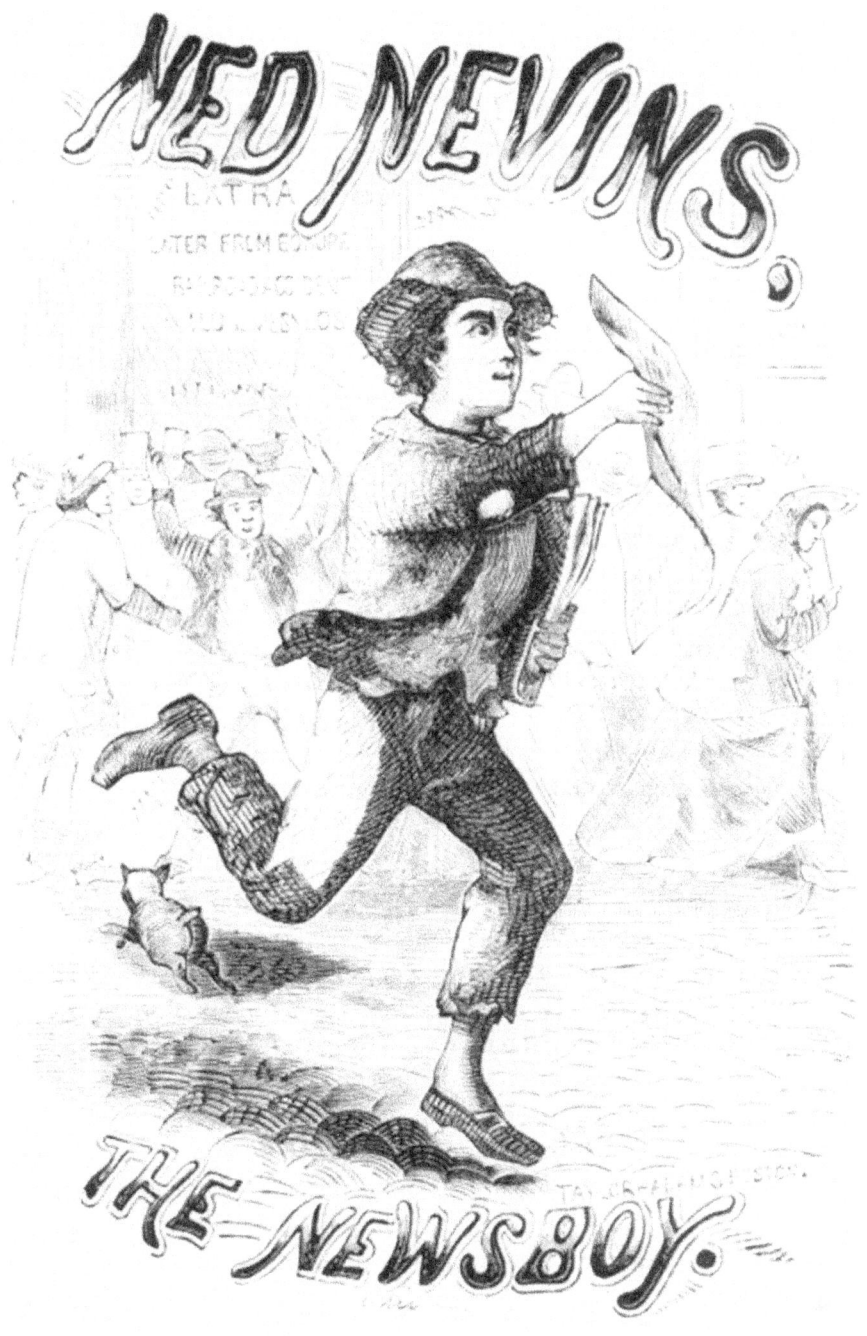

Cover of *Ned Nevins the Newsboy*, 1867.

in Paris, prompt him to call Paris the worst place he has ever been. Augustus Gildersleeve disagrees, saying that Boston is worse than Paris, for everything that Paris does in public, Boston does in secret.

This is an epiphany to Morgan, who vows to return to Boston, find out if it is true and, if so, do everything he can to stop it. In reality, Reverend Morgan had been a temperance preacher his whole adult life and hardly needed a trip to Europe to show him the evils of Boston, but the point was made.

Boston Inside Out! exposes and indicts all of the city's corrupt institutions and individuals while following two story lines so prurient that, if Morgan's motives had not been so pure, it would surely have been attacked by other moral reformers. In one storyline, Augustus Gildersleeve's son Frank has become infatuated with young Minnie Marston from rural Connecticut, but her low social status prevents him from proposing marriage. Determined to have her regardless, Frank sets out to seduce Minnie with the help of his friend, a dentist named Dr. Forceps. Forceps, a depraved man of the world, introduces Frank to the sins of Boston, taking him to faro games and Sunday saloons, coaching his progress with Minnie by suggesting he take her to suggestive plays and bribe clairvoyants to make her more receptive to his advances. When all other attempts fail, Frank has his way with Minnie in Dr. Forceps's dentist chair while she is anesthetized by ether. The result is pregnancy, abortion and ruin for Minnie Marston.

The other storyline follows a well-connected Catholic priest, Father Titus, as he seduces Rose Delaney, a young married woman in his congregation. She becomes part of his harem of "nieces." Much of the controversy around Morgan's book was driven by speculation as to who the fictional characters were meant to portray. It is clear that a fair number of the twenty-five thousand copies were sold to people not fully committed to moral reform.

Morgan very graphically indicted those he felt responsible for Boston's moral decline, by reputation if not by name. First were the wealthy aristocrats of Boston, who descended from the Puritan founders and benefited from their righteousness but turned their backs on orthodox religion. Viewing themselves as outside the law, they leased their properties for immoral purposes and engaged in all forms of debauchery. Also guilty were the police and public officials who were in the pockets of the rum interests and refused to enforce vice laws.

Morgan's descriptions of midnight "explorations into the dark ways and by-ways of Boston" with its "myriads of flashing lights" and "strains of bacchanalian song, drunken shouts and ribald laughing" could easily apply to Bose Cobb's notorious West End dance hall. Bose Cobb, a flamboyant African American saloonkeeper, operating outside the laws of God and man, had become the symbol of everything sinful in the Hub. His dance hall, denounced by reformers as the worst place in Boston, was a gateway to sin of every description and often the scene of violence, yet it flourished year after year.

At the height of the Victorian age, no person in Boston knew more about the city's sinful ways than did Bose Cobb and Reverend Henry Morgan— one from the side of the devil, one from the side of salvation. There was scarcely an aspect of vice in Boston that was not perpetrated by one or condemned by the other. Each had a role to play in the competition for the souls of righteous Bostonians. Cobb's free-and-easy invitation to vice and depravity was countered by Reverend Morgan's frenzied shouts of warning:

> *Now why do I reveal Boston's dark ways? Why expose her snares, pitfalls, and forbidden paths? It is to warn the unwary! To awaken fathers and mothers to their children's danger! To a sense of duty! To fire the pulpit with alarm! To arouse the church, the press, and public opinion! Oh! fathers and mothers, set the signal for the coming train! For your children and your children's children! For generations yet unborn! The forests are cleared, the road-bed raised, the bridge is built, yet the track is ajar! Lo, the cars are coming! Your neighbors and your neighbors' children! Oh! set the signal for the coming train! Wave the flag! Swing the lantern! Lift the voice! Sound the whistle! Ring the Bell! DOWN BRAKES! DOWN BRAKES! Danger ahead! Friends and loved ones are at the brink! Ho! To the rescue! To the rescue! Set the signal! Set the signal for the train is coming!*

Chapter 2

THE BLACK SEA

In the spring of 1858, the Reverend Perez Mason was preparing for missionary work, preaching the gospel and saving souls among the godless heathens. "This is carrying the war into Africa," wrote one newspaper, but Reverend Mason was not traveling to the Dark Continent; the quote was a reference to the Roman military strategy of attacking your enemy's home. Mason would be taking his mission to the notorious Black Sea section of Boston's North End.

In the 1840s, the Black Sea was a densely populated stretch of Ann Street between Union and Richmond Streets. Commercially, it was a low-price shopping district featuring secondhand stores, new and used furniture stores and "slop-shops"—stores selling low-priced, ready-made clothing, a business that proved to be quite profitable. Andrew Carney, a tailor who ran a slop-shop on Ann Street, was so successful that, in 1843, he paid $92,000 cash—ninety-two $1,000 bills—for the Goddard estate on Summer Street in downtown Boston and became a major real estate mogul. George W. Simmons, whose slop-shop in Oak Hall was the largest on Ann Street, would, in 1899, found Simmons College.

The low rents that attracted cut-rate retailers also attracted poor immigrants, African Americans, sailors and itinerants of every race and nationality, but it was not exactly a melting pot. Groups that were scarcely cordial in the best of circumstances were constantly at one another's throats in the crowded conditions of the Black Sea. Because of its nearness to the harbor, many sailors would stay in racially segregated Black Sea

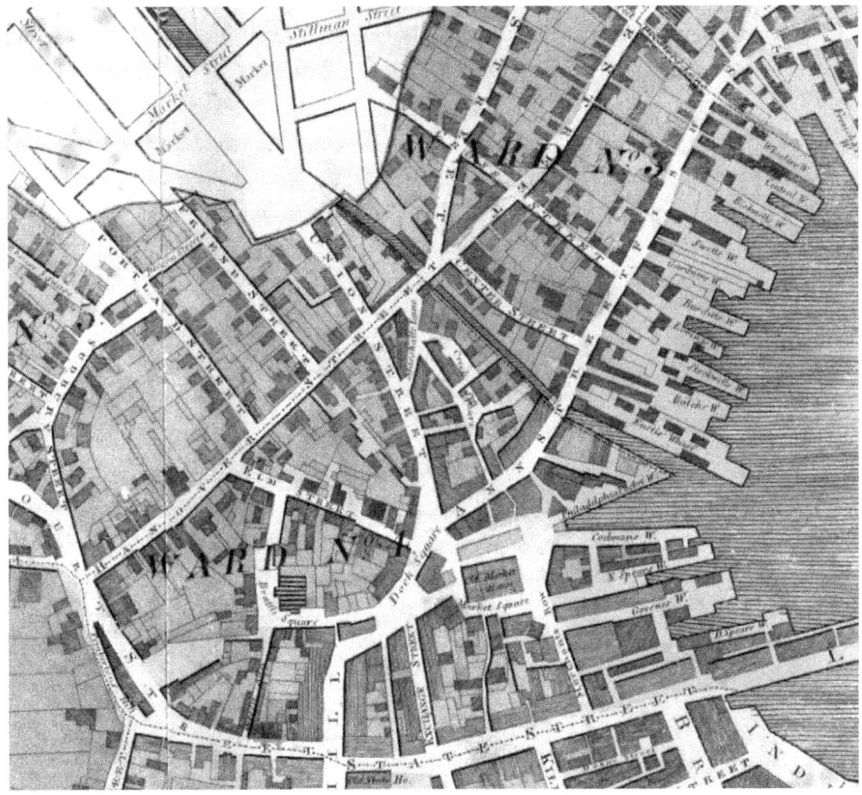

The Black Sea, 1814. *Wikimedia Commons.*

boardinghouses between voyages. One summer Sunday in 1843, a small-scale riot broke out on Ann Street when a dozen or so black boarders were blocking the sidewalk and the boatswain's mate of the USS *Ohio*, a white man, objected to walking around them. Words were exchanged and then punches were thrown; soon sailors poured out of all the boardinghouses to join the mêlée. Police were on hand, but their number was too small to break up the fight, so they rang the fire alarm and an engine full of firemen arrived, took charge of the scene and broke up the fight. Henry Foreman, who owned the black boardinghouse, came home from church to find the place in shambles, the windows broken and furniture demolished.

The residents of the Black Sea lived in crowded squalor, sometimes as many as twenty in a single windowless room, in conditions similar to those in the Five Points neighborhood in New York City. A fictionalized account printed in the *Boston Bee* in 1846, titled "Stella Lea, the Orphan Girl," depicted the dismal conditions in the Black Sea. Abandoned with her young child, Stella Lea's mother meets a man who promises to help her:

> *He finally brought the mother and child to Boston, and for several months they were the inmates of a miserable hovel in the purlieus of Ann Street. The child was now about five years old, and the angelic little being was surrounded, constantly, by the myrmidons of iniquity, old, filthy, debauched hags, and loathsome, profane, obscene devils, in the form of men; and she never knew what a pure word, or kind look, or a cleanly person was.*

When the sun went down on Ann Street, the neighborhood descended into an abyss of drunkenness and debauchery. The basements of most of the buildings housed unlicensed saloons known as rum cellars; if music and dancing were offered, they were called dance cellars. Like the retail stores above them, the rum cellars sold cut-rate merchandise. Reportedly, Patrick Cain, proprietor of one of the cellar establishments, was arrested for selling gin without a license. A young man called to testify in Cain's defense swore that he paid for and drank a glass of fluid but could not swear that it was gin.

Bad liquor was the least of the Black Sea's dangers. Many of the cellars featured games of dead props (dice) or faro that were seldom on the level. Young toughs would wait on the street for drunks to emerge from the cellars and then relieve them of whatever money they had left. But the greatest perils of Ann Street were the *nymphes du pave*, the prostitutes of every age and race, ever present in every cellar and on every street corner. They would entice a man, charge him for their services and then steal his wallet. For obvious reasons, the victims seldom reported these crimes to the police.

The police and the officials of Boston were well aware of the activities on Ann Street, but the official policy regarding vice in the Black Sea was to leave it alone unless someone filed a complaint. Complaints were followed up and acted upon, but throughout the 1840s, no move was made to break up the Black Sea or stop its illegal activities. The victims of Black Sea vice were seen as outsiders—sailors on leave, business travelers, countrymen, itinerant bums—who willingly or accidentally found themselves in a dangerous place. Said one state representative, "Who ever heard of a Boston boy being shaken down in Ann Street?"

By 1850, the nocturnal activities of the Black Sea had spilled into the daylight hours, and honest residents complained that it was no longer safe to walk down Ann Street at any time. Shoplifters plagued the retail stores, and stolen merchandise from other parts of the city began showing up in Black Sea pawnshops and secondhand stores. One man was arrested for trying to sell a crate of live chickens he had stolen from the nearby market at Faneuil Hall.

In his annual report of the police department for 1850, City Marshal Frances Tukey paid particular attention to the rising crime rate in the Black Sea. Despite the department's hands-off attitude toward the Black Sea, one officer alone that year had made 123 arrests for larcenies, robberies and burglaries; 55 for assault and battery; 30 for receiving stolen goods; and 211 for drunkenness. "In Ann Street alone," the report stated, "we are informed, there are seventy-two dance cellars, and brothels and liquor-shops almost innumerable, in which the most depraved of both sexes and all colors are constantly congregated, and robberies and assaults are so common that it is not always safe to pass through there even in the day time." In the worst places, it proved impossible to get evidence due to the character of the visitors. Even when prosecution was successful, the rum cellars, though fined again and again, were able to remain profitable.

A little before 10:00 p.m. on April 23, 1851, fifty Boston police officers and about the same number of watchmen (separate departments at the time) combined to make a "grand descent upon the haunts of vice and crime in Ann Street and vicinity." The move, ordered by the mayor and aldermen, in compliance with a recommendation from the grand jury, was so swift and sudden that the denizens of the Black Sea had no time to prepare or escape. A total of 153 men, women and girls were arrested and marched first to the Watch House on Hanover Street and then to the Leverett Street jail. A few of the 93 women arrested who had been before the court previously were sentenced directly to the house of correction. The rest were fined three dollars apiece, but few of them had that money, and they were sent to that institution as well. Of the men arrested, 35 were arraigned on outstanding indictments as brothel keepers, keepers of noisy and disorderly houses and violators of liquor license and Sunday laws. The rest were sent to police court and charged with being tipplers, vagabonds, pipe-players, fiddlers, dancers and so on.

Edward E. Savage, who would later become Boston's chief of police, was a new recruit at the time of the 1851 police descent. While impressed with the efficiency of the raid, as time went on, Savage questioned the results. The sentences of those sent to the house of correction soon expired, and with the police still watching Ann Street, the offenders had nowhere to go. They dispersed throughout the city. Some of the more presentable women

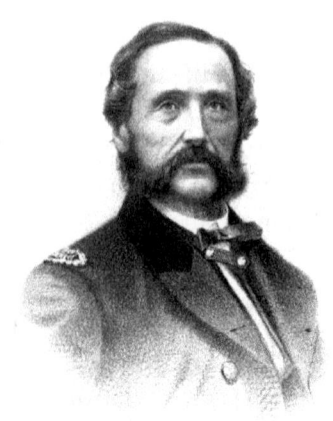

Edward Hartwell Savage. *From* Police Records and Recollections, *1873.*

found work as domestic servants, but none of them had reformed. House robberies and burglaries in Boston increased at an alarming rate.

The following year, for the benefit of businesses and respectable citizens of Ann Street, the city changed the street's name to North Street. Some poor sailor may have spent the night wandering the North End looking unsuccessfully for Ann Street, where he had had so much fun the last time his ship was harbored in Boston, but the confusion would have been short-lived. The police could not occupy the street forever, and it wasn't long before the dance cellars, gambling houses and streetwalkers returned to the Black Sea, taking up residence on North Street as if nothing had happened.

In 1858, Edward Savage, now a police captain, was entrusted to launch another police descent into the Black Sea, but he took a gentler approach than Marshal Tukey had. Savage had a sensitive side and saw the young prostitutes as victims rather than criminals. He could sympathize with their plight while others only condemned, as is shown in these verses from "Little Ragged Nell," a poem Savage wrote about a North End orphan girl he knew who had been led astray:

> *Fair jewels, soon, and gaudy silk,*
> *Will deck fair Nellie's form;*
> *In gilded halls and mazy dance,*
> *She mingles with the throng.*
> *Where vice, enshrined in mellow light,*
> *Tempting the young and fair,*
> *Bewitching cheat—heartless deceit,*
> *Wooing but to ensnare.*

> *Near by this narrow alley-way,*
> *Where little Nell was born,*
> *A church-spire rears in proud display;*
> *And on each Sabbath morn,*

The rich meet here to worship God,
Who "doeth all things well";
But no one feels or cares to pray
For little ragged Nell.

Prostitution and accompanying crimes were once again out of control in the Black Sea, and while the old stock had not diminished, officers could count fifty or sixty new faces of girls from the country among them. Savage obtained fifty-four warrants from Judge Wells of the police court, and on the night of October 22, he led forty policemen, without uniforms, to North Street. Within half an hour, fifty-one women were in custody in the guardhouse. The raid was early in the evening; the women had not yet begun their night's work. "To an unpracticed eye they might have been mistaken for an assembly of beautiful and accomplished young ladies," wrote Savage, "for they were now quite sober and reserved, rum not having had time on that night to accomplish its accursed work."

Savage spoke to each woman separately, and they all spent a night in jail. The next day in police court, each was given a strong sentence, which would be suspended for those who agreed to leave the city and return to their homes and parents. Forty-seven of the women accepted the opportunity. Captain Savage, optimist and writer of poetry, believed that they had all fulfilled their agreement and sincerely hoped that most had left these dens of infamy forever.

Reverend Mason was optimistic as well. That same year, he began his mission to the Black Sea by preaching in a notorious dance hall on North Street "to a full assemblage of miscellaneous characters." That June, he opened the North Street Independent Mission, holding well-attended daily meetings with additional meetings on Sunday and Thursday evenings. He established a Sunday school with more than one hundred pupils.

In May 1858, the North Street Independent Mission observed its first anniversary with a celebration at the Park Street Church. The executive committee reported the accomplishments of Father Mason, as he was known in the community. He had visited numerous prisoners and worked for their release; he provided aid to the sick and destitute in hospitals, jails and at home; and he distributed fifty-seven Bibles that year and over twenty thousand papers and tracts. A total of 2,400 Black Sea residents signed the temperance pledge of the mission. Sixty-five women had been won from the dens of vice and provided with respectable homes, one of whom, Mrs. Anna Cooley, stayed to work for the mission and spoke at the celebration.

The number of souls reclaimed by the police and the mission was surely impressive, but vice would remain in the Black Sea for at least another generation. Even in the unlikely condition that all the recipients of Captain Savage's suspended sentences remained happily at home with their parents, and all of Father Mason's pledgers remained sober and steered clear of the dens of vice, depravity was deeply entrenched in the Black Sea, and new, willing participants arrived daily.

By the 1870s, a variety of improvements had been made to North Street. The city widened and regraded the street and installed sewers. The once perilously dark street was now illuminated by gaslights. The rum cellars had become street-level saloons, and the streetwalkers had found homes in the North Street brothels, standing side by side with new legitimate businesses moving to North Street—and the same men owned both. "Now these are the upper-crust of society," wrote Reverend Morgan. "But upper-crusts and under-crust meet at the edges. Upper-crusts of Beacon Hill, under-crusts of North Street—one of wine the other of whiskey."

The houses of ill fame were owned by men who lived in other parts of the city, and some had become quite well known. Bose Cobb, who had begun his criminal career shortly after the Civil War running a dice game on North Street, by the 1870s owned at least one brothel there but was able to distance himself from the day-to-day operations. When police raided his house, the newspapers would report Bose Cobb as the owner, but it was the madam who would have to answer in police court.

Though never successful of ridding the Black Sea of vice or saving the souls of all its inhabitants, gradually the police succeed in raising the Black Sea from the depths of depravity. By the end of the 1870s, police raids were so frequent that even Bose Cobb decided to move his entire operation—saloon, dance hall, gambling rooms and bawdyhouses—out of the Black Sea and into the West End.

Chapter 3

BAITING RATS AND
BUCKING THE TIGER

The door of Barney Ford's saloon on North Street opened into a long, narrow room with a bar down the entire length of one wall. A bench and a few stools were scattered haphazardly across the floor, and half a dozen or so uncouth pictures decorated the walls. Behind the counter, barmaids "with vermilion cheeks and low-necked dresses" stood ready to deal out second-rate liquor and cheap cigars. Those in the know passed them by and passed by the haggard little man serving up raw oysters as well, walking all the way to the end of the bar to find a trapdoor in the floor and descend the stairs to the rat pit in the cellar.

At the bottom of the stairs, a man would pay twenty-five cents to enter a room dimly lit by a few oil lamps and candles stuck into potatoes, turnips and empty bottles. In the center of the floor was the pit—an octagonal board crib, about eight feet in diameter, the sides about three feet high. Facing three sides of the pit were rows of board seats to accommodate spectators, though the large crowd of men spent more time on their feet than seated on benches.

Barney Ford, who had a somewhat successful career as a prizefighter before opening the saloon, served as the master of ceremonies for the night's entertainment. As he approached the rat pit carrying an old flour barrel, now half full of live rats, the men began exuberantly making wagers on the event's outcome. Using a pair of tongs, Barney fished out the rats and dropped them, one by one, into the pit, as his assistant brought in the dog, Flora, a favorite ratter. He held her tight by the nape of the neck as she panted anxiously, eager for the fray.

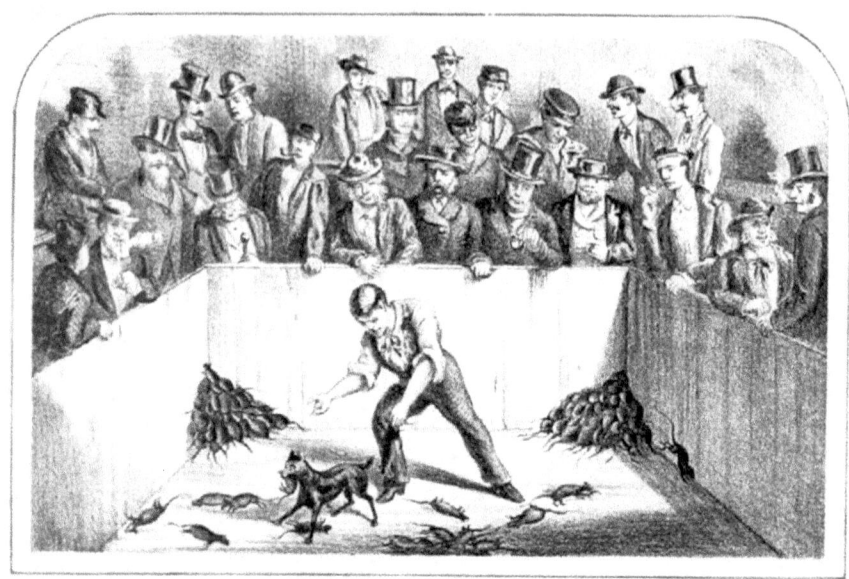

Rat pit. *From* Police Records and Recollections, *1873.*

The men were betting on how many rats Flora could kill in the allotted time, chaotically shouting numbers and amounts in a manner as frantic and incomprehensible to outsiders as trading on a stock market floor. Barney called time, the betting stopped and his assistant dropped Flora into the pit. The men cheered her on, but Flora needed little coaxing: "the growling, and champing, and squealing, is soon over." Time was called again, and twenty rats lay lifeless at Flora's feet. The bets were settled with remarkable speed and civility, and the men climbed the stairs for liquor while Barney and his assistant readied another barrel of rats and another bloodthirsty dog.

Sometimes they played the "chuck game"—a woodchuck or some similar wild animal would be placed in the pit in a box three or four feet long and one foot square, open on one end. The spectators bet on whether the dog could pull the chuck out of the box and, if so, how long it would take. In the words of Police Chief Savage, "The hooting, cheering, groaning, shouting, and stamping, accompanied with ten thousand grotesque gestures of the crowd as seen and heard by the dim light in that subterranean dungeon, beggars description, and would put to blush a pandemonium of the first water."

Rat pits, per se, were not illegal in Boston, except to the extent that all gambling was illegal, but most would keep their locations secret and move from place to place. But there were exceptions. Barney Ford's rat pit was permanent and quite well known, and Harry Jennings advertised in the *Boston Herald* that his place on Portland Street featured "A private Rat Pit and plenty of Rats always on hand."

Aside from the obvious barbarity of blood sports such as rat baiting, dogfighting and cockfighting, moralists objected to the fact that these attractions were not just for the poor and ignorant; they were frequented by higher-class gentlemen as well. A commentator in 1833 described a cockfight lasting until 4:00 a.m. where "sons of the aristocracy" mingled with Boston's lowest elements. Benjamin Crowninshield, from a Boston Brahmin family, who later became secretary of the navy under Presidents Madison and Monroe, wrote of visiting a rat pit with some of his Harvard classmates. For one night in 1870, the West End Opera House ran a rat pit in place of its usual entertainment. Admission was one dollar, but free tickets were "liberally circulated among the fanciers of genus canis, who move in official and other circles." Among the motley audience were members of the court and city government officials who happily watched the killing of some two hundred rats by half-starved dogs.

Though blood sports would continue in Boston throughout the nineteenth century, more sedate forms of gambling were far more common. Boston had a professional baseball team beginning in 1876, and with competitive sports came gambling. Pool gambling—betting on horse races, baseball games and other sports—had become a million-dollar-a-year business in Boston. To the New England Society for the Suppression of Vice, pool gambling was "one of the most common and ruinous evils of the present day." Thousands of young men who would not consider themselves gamblers made bets daily during baseball season, not just on the outcome of games but on "dos and don'ts"—the successes of certain events in separate innings.

The society identified two professional gamblers, John Reber and John Gallagher, as the main perpetrators of pool gambling in Boston, taking in thousands of dollars a day in their haunt at 15 Spring Lane, Downtown. Though it was able to press charges against Reber and Gallagher in 1885, the court determined that the law was "defective" and the gamblers could not be prosecuted. The society worked to amend the law but ran into opposition. The problem was that the proposed law would affect betting on horse races as well as baseball games, and many of the legislators could not imagine watching the trotters at Mystic Park without placing a few bets.

With the support of local businessmen, the society finally got the proposed amendments passed. Reber and Gallagher were arrested twice more in the spring of 1886, and after much strong opposition, they were finally indicted, convicted and sentenced to jail. Henry Chase, agent for the Society for the Suppression of Vice, was convinced that pool gambling had been substantially broken up in Boston and he had saved the city's young men $50,000 to $75,000 in gambling losses that year. However, it is safe to assume that the vacuum left by the incarceration of Reber and Gallagher was filled very quickly.

Saloon gambling was also a serious concern for the New England Society for the Suppression of Vice. Games such as faro, roulette and dead props were played in saloons and gambling houses throughout the city, and among criminal enterprises, none was as fast, safe and sure as a gaming table. On the other side of the table, gambling was also the fastest way for a man to ruin his life. The irrational and obsessive nature of gambling, the need to chase losses with more wagers, hoping for a change in luck, drove men to bet more money than they could afford to lose and even borrow or steal to feed their habit. This fact became obvious to the Society for the Suppression of Vice, which increasingly focused on supporting legislation to outlaw gambling and on prodding the police to enforce existing laws. The society complained that police raids on gambling houses netted few arrests, and even when proprietors were arrested, they were seldom prosecuted.

The police took a different position on gambling. As with other vice laws, the police were not proactive in their enforcement, acting only on official complaints. The majority of complaints they received were from groups like the Society for the Suppression of Vice. For most of the century, the laws themselves made enforcement difficult. A complaint was not sufficient; the police had to catch a game in progress. Even if they found gambling paraphernalia—roulette wheels, chips, table layouts and so on—it was not enough evidence to assume that the law had been broken. They would confiscate or destroy the equipment but could not arrest the owners. Some gambling houses employed sentries to warn the house if the police were approaching, but most simply installed iron doors and barred windows and made players give a password to enter. Even if the police decided to break down the door, the house had plenty of time to hide the equipment; the law would enter to find a group of men smoking cigars and peacefully conversing.

The society also accused the police of taking bribes from gambling houses and giving them advance notice of raids. They were not wrong in this; gambling houses offered the police officers a great opportunity to take payoffs simply to let the houses know when a raid was coming. Police chiefs were well aware of the situation and would occasionally shuffle captains among different divisions to upset the status quo. The effect was always short-lived. The only times gambling raids proved fruitful was when the orders came directly from the chief and the targets remained a secret to everyone below until the absolute last minute.

Reverend Morgan encouraged those with large gambling losses to bypass the police and threaten those who ran the houses with suits in civil court. He assisted by publishing the names of people behind the big gambling houses and claimed some major successes in reclaiming gambling losses. He wrote of several cases where a man or his son, usually while under the influence of alcohol, lost more than he could afford but, upon presenting the gamblers with the facts and threatening a lawsuit, got his money back without cost or risk of exposure.

Unofficially, the police offered the same service for their high-end constituents. In the 1860s, Chief of Police Colonel John Kurtz handed any recovery cases over to Detectives Jones and Heath, who were accomplished at meeting with gamblers and arranging "compromises." It was implied that the compromises included the financial betterment of Jones and Heath, as well as the complainant. The willingness of the police to compromise with gamblers was well known to insiders but was kept a secret from the public. Even the press kept it quiet until 1870, when the money involved was $10,000 embezzled from the city treasury and several newspapers took issue with Colonel Kurtz seeking a compromise solution.

Most Boston gambling "hells" had little to fear from Reverend Morgan's lawsuits or the compromises of Detectives Jones and Heath. For small-time houses, steel doors and iron bars were all the protection they needed from arrest or retribution. But sometimes the metal barriers proved more of a hindrance than a help. Such was the case for Lanahan and Flanigan, two old-time gamblers who ran a faro bank on Avery Street, Downtown.

The game of faro, commonly associated with gambling houses in the old West, was also the most popular game in eastern cities. It was simple to learn, easy to set up and break down and appealed to beginners and veteran gamblers alike. The layout consists of an entire suit of cards (usually spades) from ace to king, printed on green felt. "Bucking the tiger," as playing faro was called, involves the player placing chips on one or more card in the layout. On each turn, the dealer draws one losing card and one winning card. Those betting on the winning card double their money; those betting on the losing card lose their money. All other bets are unaffected. If both cards are the same denomination, the house takes half the chips bet on that

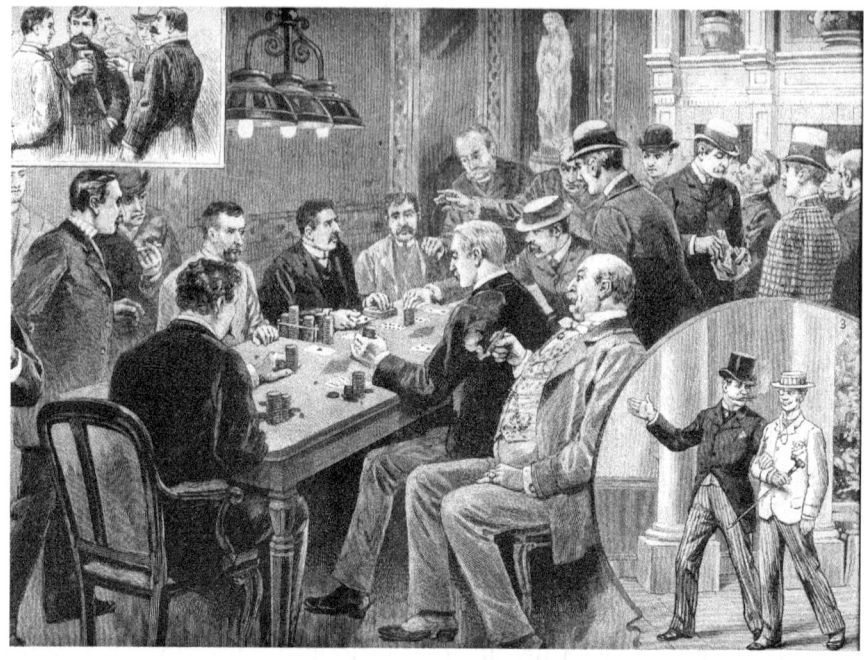

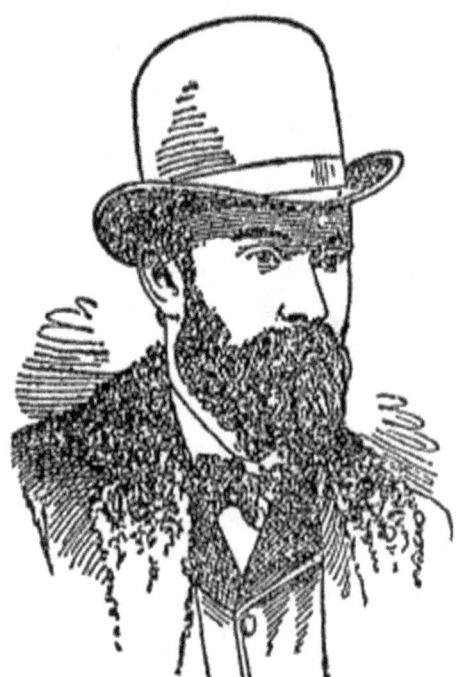

Above: A faro game, 1889. *Wikimedia Commons.*

Left: Dr. Adolph Albrecht. *From* Boston Daily Globe, *March 31, 1887.*

card. The cards already dealt are tracked on a chalkboard or a casekeep—a device resembling an abacus—for all to see. The house advantage in faro is very small; in a fair game, the player's odds are close to fifty-fifty. But the games were seldom fair.

The faro bank at 10 Avery Street run by David Lanahan, known as the "Dude Gambler," and white-haired Edward Flanigan was a "brace" game—i.e., a game explicitly run to cheat the players. Of course, Adolph Albrecht was not aware of this when he entered 10 Avery to buck the tiger on March 29, 1887. Dr. Albrecht was a young Boston druggist, a single man of good character, not known to be a habitual gambler. He probably stopped in for a little fun before going home.

Business had been slow for Lanahan and Flanigan due to the increasing frequency of police raids. It is not likely that the men feared arrest—sixty-year-old Flanigan had two sons, one on the police force and one a clerk in city hall—but raids slowed down business for everyone.

When Albrecht came in, the gamblers were determined to fleece him. Lanahan dealt while Flanigan kept track of the cards. The play was quiet, without the usual distractions surrounding a game of faro. Albrecht was not drinking, and he was the only man playing. He put five dollars on the queen and watched closely as Lanahan dealt. Albrecht saw Lanahan deal two cards at a time; he began swearing and grabbed his bet from the table.

"You sneak, I will make you give up the money," said Lanahan as he jumped up and grabbed an iron bar used to fasten the windows. He struck Albrecht in the head.

Bleeding profusely from the head wound, Albrecht drew a .38-caliber Smith & Wesson revolver from his pocket and shot Lanahan where he stood.

Flanigan grabbed a bar of iron and ran to Albrecht, saying, "I'll kill you for that."

Fearing for his life, Albrecht fired again, putting a bullet through Flanigan's jaw, but he kept coming. He fired again, but wild with rage, Flanigan kept coming, raining blows on Albrecht, trying to kill him. Albrecht kept firing; one bullet hit Flanigan's neck, another his chest, until finally he grew weak from loss of blood, threw down the bar and staggered to the door. Blinded by the blood streaming from his wounds, he fell headlong down the stairs.

The gunshots attracted a crowd on the street outside, and two officers arrived on the scene but could not get into the building because of the iron door and barred windows. One officer found a window he could smash through, and the other climbed to the roof and found a skylight protected by an iron grate. He jumped on the grating until he fell through onto the attic floor below. Albrecht, still holding the smoking revolver, surrendered to the police. Flanigan lay groaning at the foot of the stairs, calling for an ambulance. He died in the hospital that night, cursing Albrecht with his dying breath.

Adolph Albrecht was charged with willful murder and held without bail. The following June, the charge was reduced to two counts of manslaughter, and Albrecht pleaded guilty. He was sentenced to four years at hard labor.

Newspapers in Boston and elsewhere referred to the Avery Street case in editorials on the need to outlaw the use of iron doors and to give the police the power to arrest even if a game is not in progress. The police and the Society for the Suppression of Vice pressured the state legislature to make the presence of the paraphernalia and implements of gambling prima facie evidence of the crime. Later that year, though gambling interests spent thousands of dollars to defeat it, the measure was passed.

Chapter 4

THE GUILTY THIRD TIER

*A*ctress Olive Logan, writing in 1870, recalled standing on the stage as a young girl looking up at the pandemonium, "the brutal exhibition of faces," in the theater's upper gallery. "That dark, horrible, guilty 'third tier!' How dreadful it seemed to me that the theater should be cursed with such a monstrous inequity!" The "third tier" was an old theater tradition of setting aside the highest section of the balcony for the sole use of prostitutes to solicit and ply their trade. In the 1840s, the third tier was a regular fixture of theaters in every city in America, and Boston was no exception. For those who felt the theater was inherently immoral, as most of Boston's clergy did, the charge against the third tier was an argument that their opponents could not refute.

Arguments against the morality of the theater were more common and more vehement in Boston than in other American cities because of the city's Puritan ancestors, who abhorred everything about the theater. In 1687, Increase Mather, a Puritan leader of the Massachusetts Bay Colony, wrote:

> *Stage-Plays had their Original from those Devil-Gods whom the Gentiles Worshiped. The Infernal Spirits did expressly command that men should use Recreations, which we may be sure they would never have done, were not such Pastimes displeasing to God and dangerous to the Souls of Men.... Hence, Ancients call such Theaters, the Devils Temples, Stage Plays, the Devils Lectures, And the Actors in them the Devils chief Factors.*

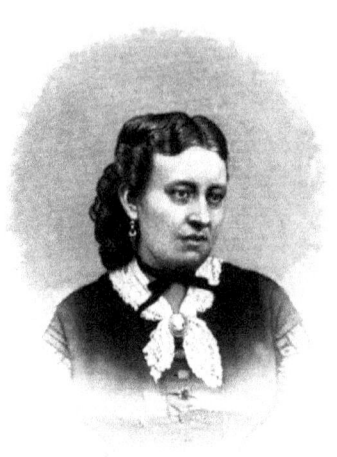 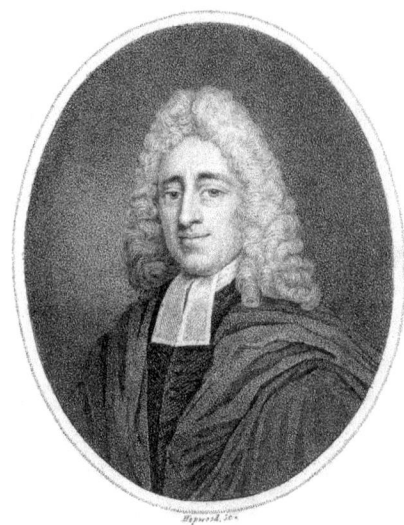

Left: Olive Logan. *From* Before the Footlights and Behind the Scenes, *1870.*

Right: Increase Mather. *Wikimedia Commons.*

The Puritans in Boston were intolerant of any form of amusement—art, music, holiday celebrations, dancing and inappropriate clothing were not allowed. Stage plays were unthinkable, and even church services were stripped of all theatrical elements and anything that might stimulate emotion and detract from the sermon.

In 1750, while the Puritans had become Congregationalists and were joined in Boston by Baptists, Methodists and Catholics, the ban on theater was still in effect. A coffeehouse presented a two-man play that year, setting off riots that resulted in legislation to further restrict the theater. The law was finally repealed in 1793; theaters were built and plays produced, but the controversy did not subside. In 1796, British actors ridiculing the French at the Haymarket Theater led to a riot between pro-British and pro-French factions in the audience, and in 1798, a fire in the Haymarket Theater was seen by the righteous as an act of God's displeasure.

In Victorian Boston, the theater was generally, if not universally, accepted. As a further slap in the face to their detractors, Boston theaters had all instituted a third tier. William Dunlap, one of the first historians of the American theater, commented on Boston's third tiers:

It is to be lamented that when the people of Massachusetts introduced the theater in their capital, having the experience of the world before them, they had not set an example to fellow citizens by purifying the dramatic establishments and abolishing this evil. They appear to have noticed it, but instead of remedying, they, if possible, made it worse.

Boston's two biggest theaters in the 1840s, the Boston Theater and the Tremont Theater, presented Shakespeare's plays as well as contemporary dramas, featuring the finest actors of the day. It was understood, if left unspoken, that they also provided a third tier populated by prostitutes and their clients.

The women were expected to arrive at the theater at least an hour before the performance and enter through a separate entrance in the back so as not to be seen by the regular theatergoers. Their customers would enter through the regular entrance and find their way to the third tier from inside the theater. When business was slow, sometimes the women would leave the third tier and cruise other parts of the audience looking for customers. After the meeting, some customers would leave with the prostitute and follow her to her brothel; others might prefer to make an evening of it, dining together and then finishing the night at some quiet house of assignation. Those less particular and more anxious would consummate the transaction without leaving the third tier.

Everyone was aware of what went on in the third tier, but few spoke of it. Newspapers might mention the third tier with a knowing wink. A reviewer in 1835, after giving a negative assessment of an actor's performance, qualified his remarks by saying, "We found ourselves in the third tier, dovetailed between two ladies, dressed quite thin considering the cold weather, and surrounded by a judge or two—several distinguished lawyers—a dozen members of Congress, on their way to Washington—some merchants in good credit—and a few religious persons, who only visit the theater on great occasions." In 1840, the *Philadelphia Public Ledger* printed the following, probably tongue-in-cheek, report: "Judicial Decision,—A judge in Boston has decided that no respectable man can possibly enter into and emerge from the third tier of a theater, and that if he goes into such a sky parlor respectable, he comes out shorn of all his respectability."

Alcohol was usually served at a bar somewhere near the third tier, contributing to the rowdiness and disturbance that proved distracting to regular customers. Sometimes theater managers would bow to public pressure and close down the third tier, but profits fell off miserably during these performances. Attendance generated by the third tier was essential to keeping many theaters afloat, and sometimes they would send blocks of tickets to brothels to draw the women and their paying customers into the theater.

In 1846, the mayor and aldermen of Boston held hearings on the question of imposing more stringent restrictions on the city's theaters. The proposal was to impose the following conditions on the licensing of theaters:

1. *There should be no separate entrance to the third tier*
2. *No female shall be allowed to enter the theater unattended by a man*
3. *Neither girls nor boys shall be admitted unattended by a parent or guardian*
4. *Police officers in the theaters shall be selected by the city authorities, and change after short periods of service*
5. *No refreshments of any kind shall be allowed to be sold in the theater.*

The attorney for the Boston Theater objected, saying that the law would not exclude women of a certain class because "there was no woman so abandoned that she could not find a more abandoned pimp to go with her to the theater; and nothing would be gained to the cause of good morals or public decency by allowing them to sit on the same benches with the respectable portion of the audience." But the ordinance was passed as written by the city council, and a fee was levied for theater licenses to pay for a police officer to attend each performance. The result meant reduced revenue and additional costs for Boston theaters.

The managers of the Tremont Theater, who were committed to quality drama, had in 1839 already implemented many of the points outlined in the new ordinance, closing the bar and third tier and refusing admission to unaccompanied women. They struggled financially for the next four years and then, in December 1843, closed the doors of the theater and sold the building to the Baptist Church.

It was considered a triumph of the church over the devil when the Baptists bought the Tremont Theater and renamed it the Tremont Temple. The dedication of the Tremont Temple was attended by prominent clergymen of every denomination, including the Reverend Henry Ward Beecher of Brooklyn, the most powerful Protestant minister in America. Beecher had long railed against the theater in language reminiscent of Increase Mather, 150 years earlier:

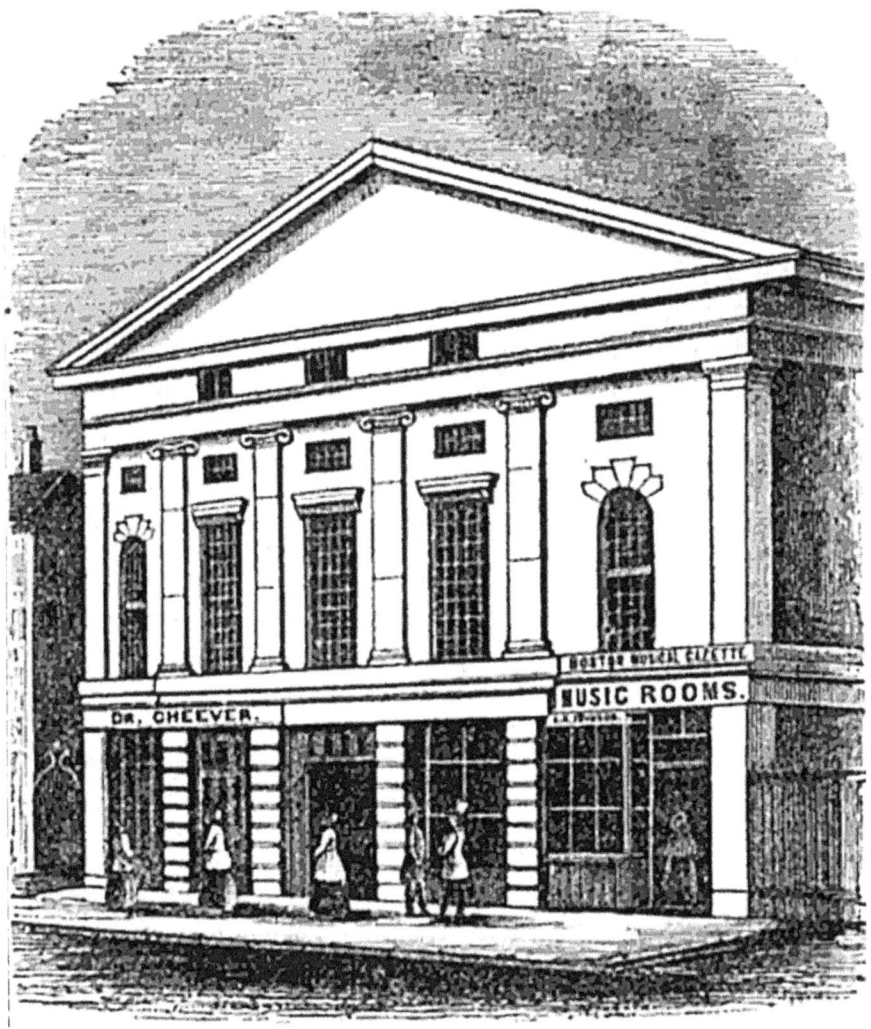

Tremont Temple. *From* Boston Directory, *1851.*

> *It is through this infamous place that the young learn to love those vicious associates and practices which, else, they would have been strangers. Half the victims of the gallows and of the penitentiary will tell you, that these schools for morals were to them the gate of debauchery, the porch of pollution, the vestibule of the very house of Death.*

The Reverend Mr. Colver, pastor of the Tremont Temple, wrote a hymn for the dedication that was sung by the choir:

Within these ransom'd walls we bow;
Too long abused to sin and shame,
To Thee we consecrate them now!
Satan has here held empire long—
A blighting curse—a cruel reign—
By mimic scenes, and mirth and song,
Alluring souls to endless pain.

Not long after the Tremont Theater became the Tremont Temple, a transaction in the West End went in the other direction: a house of worship became a theater. In the early 1840s, William Miller, through meticulous biblical research, had determined that Christ would return and the world would end on March 21, 1844 (later revised to October 21, 1844). Miller was a charismatic speaker who preached his message throughout New England and New York, and as the end of the world drew near, Miller had more than ten thousand followers. In Boston, the Millerites met in a one-story wooden tabernacle on Howard Street that could seat four thousand people. When October 21, 1844, passed uneventfully, the sect broke up, and the remaining Millerites, to cover expenses, leased out the tabernacle to a theatrical company.

On October 13, 1845, the Howard Athenaeum—named to project an air of intellectual elevation and avoid the stigma associated with the word "theater"—opened with a production of *School for Scandal*. After a fire destroyed the original structure in February 1846, two entrepreneurs—Mr. Boyd and Mr. Beard—purchased the property and had a new theater built of granite. The reopened Howard Athenaeum would be the first theater in Boston to have cushioned seats and would not include a bar or a third tier. It was, however, built over a brewery, and a nearby saloon provided refreshments between acts.

The owners had planned to concentrate on serious drama, and most of the great actors of the era trod the boards at the Howard Athenaeum—Junius Booth, William McReady, Edwin Forest, Charlotte Cushman and may more. But tastes in entertainment were rapidly changing, and before long, the Howard featured variety acts as well, such as the equestrian performance of Mrs. Virginia Sherwood in Joe Pentland's circus. As sex disappeared from the third tier, it began to show up on stage in the form of risqué comedians and dancing girls in pink tights, and "leg shows" became the rage. Before long, the Howard began to offer the fare that would make it famous: vaudeville and burlesque.

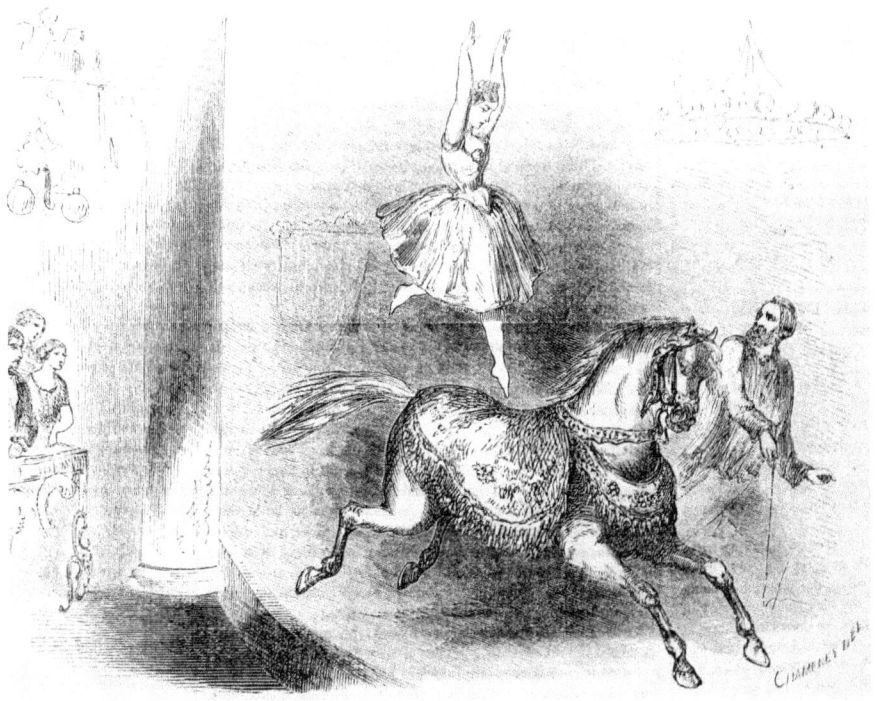

"Mrs. Sherwood, at the Howard Athenaeum." *From* Gleason's Pictorial Drawing-Room Companion, *December 23, 1854.*

In the 1880s, the theatrical world was once again in the crosshairs of social reformers. The Society for the Suppression of Vice objected not only to scantily clad actresses on stage but also the posters used to advertise them and worked to have them removed. In response to the argument that they just captured the reality of what is seen in every theater, the society responded, "We think, however that parents who wish to educate their children through other agencies than the worst features of the modern theater have a right to protest against having the ballet thrust upon them in the street."

Reformers viewed the theater as a direct opposition to the church, as a gateway to sin tempting young people to take their first steps to ruin. Reverend Morgan, in *Boston Inside Out!*, describes the seductive power of the theater on Minnie Marston when Frank Gildersleeve takes the innocent country girl to her first play. The curtains open, and Minnie is first dazzled by the light and color:

Then came a burst of music, a hush of expectation on the part of the audience, and the princess, attended by a numerous train of female attendants, entered, almost as devoid of apparel as the first inhabitants of Eden. A storm of applause greeted them. But a blush mounted on Minnie's cheek. The actions, the postures, the fantastic pirouetting, the suggestive, even wanton gestures, shocked and horrified the delicate mind of the young girl. For an instant, she gazed in wonder on the scene, and then quickly averted her burning face.

Appalled by what she sees, Minnie pleads with Frank to take her out of the theater. Frank convinces her to stay, and in spite of herself, Minnie becomes engrossed in the play—the trap is sprung.

Thus the pure, the beautiful, the innocent Minnie Marston, far from the protection of her country home, bereft of the influence of parents, church, and friends took her first lesson in the wiles of city life. Took her first steps on the pleasant pathway of temptation.

Will she awake to the peril? Or will her unwary feet be tangled in those snares ever set for the unsuspecting? Snares that lure to the dark waters of sensuality, at last, to overwhelm in sin, sorrow, and despair.

Chapter 5

OBSCENITY

In the summer of 1887, three professional photographers—Edwin R.W. Gertz, Thomas R. Burnham and Elmer Chickering—were arrested in Boston for producing and selling obscene photographs. The postcard-sized pictures, "of the worst character possible," were produced in their studios and surreptitiously sold on the streets and in the back rooms of saloons. The photographs of Elmer Chickering, the city's premier portrait photographer, were particularly noteworthy. The *New York Herald* wrote that Chickering's nudes were "prized highly by the dudes, and sold recently for prices ranging from twenty-five cents to $5 apiece" at a time when a laborer earned about $8 for a sixty-hour week.

The Boston Police did not commonly make arrests for dirty pictures. They viewed their role as limited to keeping the peace, and though the pictures were illegal, it was not the sort of crime the police actively pursued. As with so many of the offenses targeted by anti-vice crusaders, the police would not take action against obscenity unless a citizen made a formal complaint, and by their nature, obscene pictures were enjoyed in secret, away from those who might complain. The charges against these three photographers were brought by the New England Society for the Suppression of Vice, an organization with the desire and wherewithal to actively investigate obscenity.

Founded in 1878 as an offshoot of Anthony Comstock's New York Society for the Suppression of Vice, the mission of the New England Society was to combat the growing problem of indecency in books, pictures and theatrical performances, particularly regarding their influence on impressionable children. In May of that year, between four and five hundred men gathered at the Park Street Church, long a center of reform movements, to inaugurate the new society. Women were barred from the meeting, as the discussion was deemed unfit for delicate ears.

The key speaker, Anthony Comstock, spoke of his own anti-vice campaign. In addition to being the founder of the New York Society for the Suppression of Vice, Comstock served as a special agent for the post office and was instrumental in passing federal laws that bear his name. The Comstock laws passed by Congress in 1873 called for "Suppression of Trade

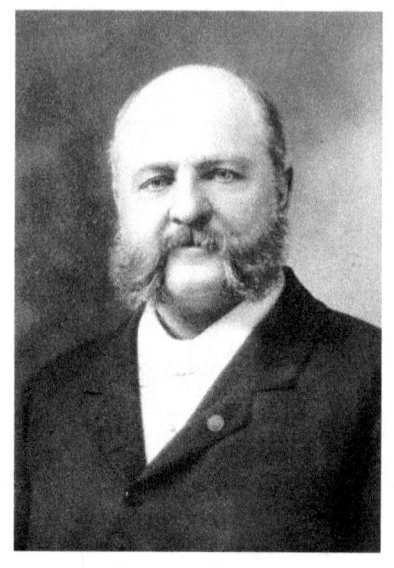

Anthony Comstock. *Wikimedia Commons.*

in, and Circulation of, Obscene Literature and Articles of Immoral Use." In his enforcement, Comstock interpreted the law very broadly, and in addition to items commonly viewed as obscene, Comstock brought charges against anyone sending literature on birth control or sexual education.

Before the foundation of the New England Society, Comstock had already been at work suppressing vice in Boston. In November 1877, he arrested Ezra Heywood, an outspoken anarchist and advocate of free love, at a convention meeting of the New England Free Love League at Boston's Nassau Hall. Heywood was one of the founders of the Free Love League and, together with his wife, Angela, published a magazine called *The Word*, with articles on free love, feminism and sexuality. They also sold books and pamphlets through the magazine. Comstock set up a sting operation, ordering two books from Heywood under the name E. Edgewall at an address in New Jersey. To Anthony Comstock, sending books on sexuality from Massachusetts to New Jersey was a violation of federal postal regulations and had to be punished.

The books ordered by Comstock were *Sexual Psychology* by R.T. Trall and Heywood's own *Cupid's Yoke*, a twenty-three-page pamphlet that argued for the abolition of marriage, calling it a social contract that made a woman into a "prostitute for life." The pamphlet caught Comstock's attention because it referred to vice suppression groups as a danger to individual freedom and criticized Anthony Comstock by name.

Ezra Heywood was tried in Boston the following January on the charge of mailing obscene publications. The trial was swift; the judge did not allow the pamphlets to be read in court and did not allow any discussion on free speech or the legality of obscenity laws. Sentencing was delayed pending appeal. The appeal, which called the Comstock laws a violation of the First Amendment, was denied after the U.S. Supreme Court, in a separate case, upheld the constitutionality of the laws. Heywood was fined $100 and sentenced to two years in Dedham jail.

Heywood's supporters continued to lobby for his release. They convinced the U.S. attorney general, Charles Devlin, that *Cupid's Yoke* was not obscene, and on Devlin's recommendation, President Hayes pardoned Ezra Heywood in December 1878.

This did not end the feud between Comstock and Heywood. In 1883, Comstock arrested Heywood again for mailing *Cupid's Yoke* and two of Walt Whitman's poems and for advertising a contraceptive vaginal douching syringe, which Heywood called the "Comstock Syringe." This time, the judge allowed Heywood to discuss the topic of obscenity in his trial, and the jury found him not guilty.

Throughout Ezra Heywood's trials and incarcerations, Angela Heywood took charge of *The Word* with articles on health, hygiene and sexual matters, eschewing Victorian euphemism and writing with extraordinary frankness.

While Comstock openly referred to Angela as the foulest of the foul-mouthed women discussing sexuality and women's rights, he never arrested her. Instead, he arrested Ezra for the sins of both. Comstock arrested Ezra Heywood twice more, and in 1890, Heywood was sentenced to two years' hard labor at Charlestown State Prison. This time, there was no pardon, and at age sixty-two, he served his sentence sewing buttons on prison uniforms. Ezra Heywood died a year after his release from prison.

Anthony Comstock viewed himself as the center of the anti-vice movement; he expected the subsidiary groups to follow his lead and to send extra funds to support his work in New York. Comstock's expectations did not sit well with the New England Society for the Suppression of Vice, and within four years, it had severed its ties with Comstock and become an independent organization.

The Boston-based society presented a more refined face than Comstock's group. The officers included popular ministers, such as Reverend Frederick Bayles Allen and Reverend Edward Everett Hale, and educators, including the presidents of Dartmouth College, Colby University, Yale College, Brown University and the University of Vermont. The agent in charge of operations

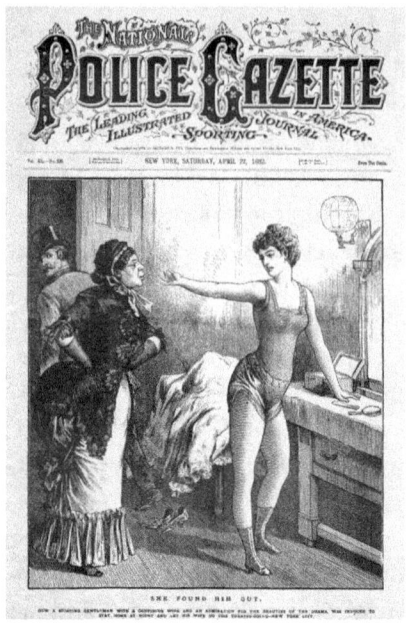

Cover of the *National Police Gazette*, April 22, 1882. *Author's collection.*

was Henry Chase, a former teacher, librarian and state representative. The list of supporting members of the society included the finest families in Boston.

The group had some early victories focusing on periodicals that it felt were harmful to children, particularly popular dime novels, with their lurid covers and stories filled with violent action glorifying gunfighters and outlaws like Jesse James. The epitome of objectionable publications was the *National Police Gazette*, which featured illustrated stories of all forms of violence and scandal interspersed with pictures of half-naked prizefighters and chorus girls in tights, often on the paper's cover. The *Police Gazette* was displayed in newsstands, in plain sight of impressionable children. At the society's urging, newsstands in Boston's train stations voluntarily stopped selling objectionable publications.

Throughout the city itself, however, newsstands did not play along, and the society had no legal means of forcing them. It also had little success with other forms of "commercialized vice," such as advertisements in store windows "pandering to man's lowest tastes" and theatrical posters featuring actresses and dancers in immodest attire. Particularly troubling were promotional pictures given away with the purchase of certain brands of cigarettes and other tobacco products featuring famous actresses scantily attired. They were easily passed from person to person, often ending up in the hands of children.

The society also went after objectionable literature, both classic and contemporary, consulting with the state's attorney to outlaw the sale of works by Boccaccio and Balzac. It was particularly hard on Walt Whitman and appealed to his publisher to censor the content of *Leaves of Grass*. In 1882, society president Homer Sprague wrote in the magazine *Education*:

> *Next come the dirt-eaters, each rolling before him his darling morsel of literary filth; disgusted with artificialities and linen decencies, and finding*

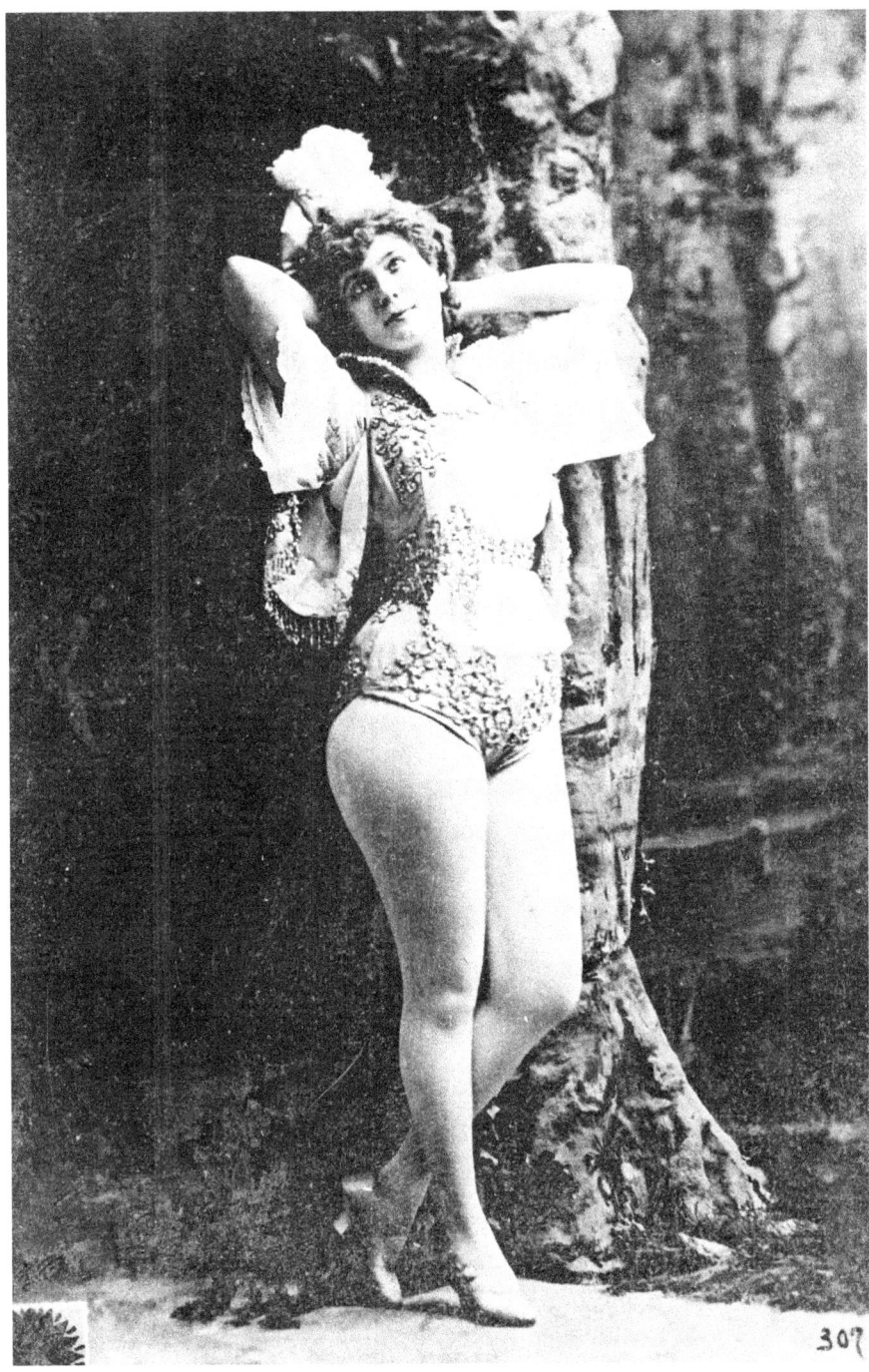

A cigarette card. *Author's collection.*

nutriment in "Leaves of Grass," but not in fig-leaves; so much in love with Nature that, like the poor human earth-worms in Xenophon, they wish to do in public what others do in private, [and] *abolish all laws against indecent exposure.*

To facilitate the fight, the New England Society for the Suppression of Vice worked to strengthen the state laws against obscenity and believed that it was making progress in the Massachusetts Statehouse. The existing obscenity law banned printed material that "contained language obscene, indecent or impure." In 1880, the society succeeded in adding the phrase "or manifestly tending to the corruption of the morals of youth" to broaden the scope of the law from just obscene language to anything that might lead to the demoralization of young people. But when the new law was enacted in 1882, the word "or" had somehow disappeared. The new law read "contained language obscene, indecent or impure, manifestly tending to the corruption of the morals of youth." Losing the "or" before "manifestly" took the teeth out of the amendment; the additional phrase now described the obscene language without adding to what was actually illegal. The society began to realize, as Reverend Morgan had, that the authorities were not exactly on their side in the fight against vice.

In their annual report for 1887, the New England Society for the Suppression of Vice proudly cited its work in the arrest and conviction of the photographers who had produced and sold obscene photographs. Twenty-five photographs and 270 negatives were seized from the photographers' studios. Edwin Gertz pleaded guilty to the charge and was fined $125 and costs. Thomas Burnham, on the same plea, was sentenced to one year in the house of correction.

But the report made no mention of Elmer Chickering. In fact, the circumstances around Chickering's case stole the thunder from the society's arrests and for a time made Boston morality the butt of jokes throughout America. In the autumn of 1886, half a dozen or so young ladies living on Commonwealth Avenue, daughters of the city's preeminent families and devotees of fine art, decided to have themselves photographed, posed in emulation of famous works of art, completely nude or thinly veiled. As a well-known portrait photographer who had photographed many famous actresses as well as most of Boston's prominent society women, Elmer Chickering was their natural choice. Chickering, who was also an oil painter and a master of composition in his photography, probably undertook the project with enthusiasm, viewing the enterprise as the girls did, as artistic

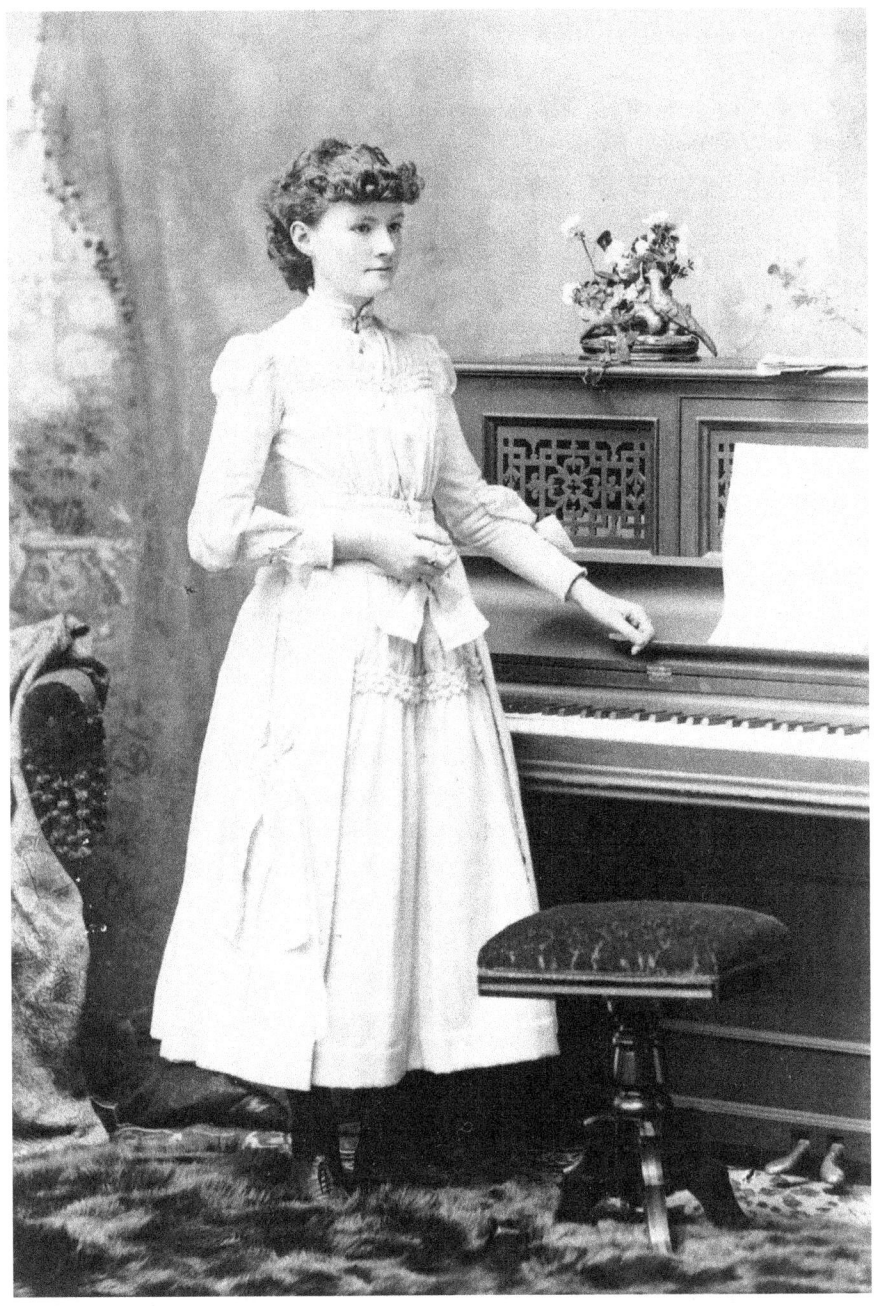

A portrait by Elmer Chickering. *Author's collection.*

rather than prurient. He took full-length pictures of individual girls posing to resemble painting such as *Venus Rising from the Sea* and sculptures such as *The Greek Slave*, as well as elaborate group shots to re-create paintings such as *Diana and Her Nymphs Bathing*.

Nude photography grew into a fad among Boston girls that fall and winter, and by some estimates, as many as fifty young women from Boston's elite Back Bay neighborhood posed *au naturel* for Elmer Chickering. Edwin Gertz in his South Boston studio provided the same service for young women not so high on the social ladder. Shop girls, factory girls and servants went to Gertz and posed, like their Back Bay sisters, reenacting famous paintings from the Paris Salon, portrayed as nymphs, goddesses and mermaids. Like those from Back Bay, the South Boston girls saw nothing wrong with the pictures. "To the pure all things are pure," one girl told reporters, "and it is only the depraved imagination of the police authorities that discovers anything wrong in their doings." The South Boston subjects intended the pictures for their private enjoyment, but Gertz had made copies to sell.

Though the Boston photographs were by far the most notorious, the nude photography fad was apparently taking hold throughout America in the 1880s. In an 1888 newspaper article, author William S.E. Fales commented:

> *The latest fad, or rather "craze" (for nothing in the long list of fashion's freaks has ever shown such a total and meaningless disregard of the social proprieties), is photographing "in the nude." Women, favored with wealth, beauty and seeming respectability repair to a trustworthy photographer or induce an amateur with an instantaneous camera to picture their limbs, chest, back, torso or entire form and then keep the tell-tale views of their folly for their own pleasure or give them to confidantes of their sex or intimates of the other.*

The Back Bay ladies had the pictures taken for their own amusement and for the admiration of a few close friends. They believed that the photographs demonstrated the high level of culture they had attained, for "a cultured mind clothes the nude human form with refined raiment which banishes all thoughts of immodesty." However, the girls apparently felt that their families had not reached the same level of culture and had the photographs sent to their houses under their servants' names. In some cases, the envelopes were returned as "addressee unknown," and the girls went back to Chickering's studio and blushingly retrieved their proofs. Reportedly, one envelope was opened by the girl's father, who, struck by the form to the exclusion of the face, did not recognize his daughter and put the photograph away in his desk for later perusal. The girl managed to get possession of the picture before her dad could get a better look.

Despite efforts to keep them secret, photographs of the Back Bay belles began to circulate outside the intimate circles for which they were intended. It was not a safe time to be producing nude photographs in Boston for any reason, with the Society for the Suppression of Vice on the lookout for anything that might corrupt the city's youth. In the spring of 1887, one of Chickering's subjects, probably encouraged by a disgruntled ex-employee, threatened to take her photograph to the police unless Chickering paid her $500. Chickering refused to be blackmailed, and on June 6, he was arrested for making and having in his possession obscene pictures.

The courtroom was packed when Chickering was brought to trial in July; rumors had spread that nude photographs of Boston's finest young ladies would be offered in evidence. But by the date of the trial, all those pictures had somehow disappeared, and the judge would rule after viewing, behind closed doors, a single photograph of a girl of lesser rank. The picture did not include the photographer's name, and according to the *Boston Globe*, there was even disagreement over whether it was a photograph of a live model or of an oil painting. Chickering focused on the blackmail story and adamantly refused to release the names of any of his models, saying, "I have no admissions and no denials and don't mean to. If the grand jury bring in an indictment I have a very good defense without telling anything about my patrons or the pictures."

The families of the girls had so much clout that few Boston newspapers covered Chickering's arrest or hearing, and those that did stuck closely to the facts presented in court. There was no mention in the Boston press of Chickering's high-society subjects, but newspapers throughout the country had great fun with the story under headlines like "As Greek Goddesses," "Beautiful Boston Girls Photographed as Nature Made Them" and "Too Too High Art."

Though exposing the city of Boston to national ridicule for a time, the story was soon forgotten. Elmer Chickering was never brought to trial, and the incident did little to damage his career. He remained the portraitist of choice for Boston's elite.

Chapter 6

THE SOCIAL EVIL

*O*fficer Hogan of the Boston Police, Third Division, accompanied by several other policemen, paid a call on the house at 52 Pitts Street in the West End on November 4, 1885, looking for a young girl named Lizzie Merchant. No. 52 Pitts was well known to the police as a house of ill repute, and when none of the inmates (as the newspapers called the women living in the house) had any information on Lizzie Merchant, the policemen undertook a search of the house.

Hogan was acting on a tip given to him by Lizzie Barry, who had recently been arrested on the charge of being idle and disorderly—probably soliciting prostitution. In 1885, the Boston Police did not tolerate streetwalkers but had a long-standing policy of ignoring prostitution when quietly practiced behind closed doors. This was a pragmatic attempt to control a practice that the police knew could not be stopped, but it did not always satisfy those with homes and businesses near the brothels. In 1825, residents and merchants of Prince Street, in the North End, rose up against a brothel known as the Beehive and burned it to the ground. Soon after, the police suppressed a similar riot at the Tin Pot on Ann Street.

In the 1880s, the center of vice in Boston was the West End, where few in the neighborhood cared about prostitutes in their midst, and the police left the houses alone. This practice, known as "segregated vice," was common in most American cities, but moral reformers found it appalling that the police knowingly allowed the illegal behavior to continue. Agents of the Society for the Suppression of Vice, who viewed the social evil as "first in the catalogue

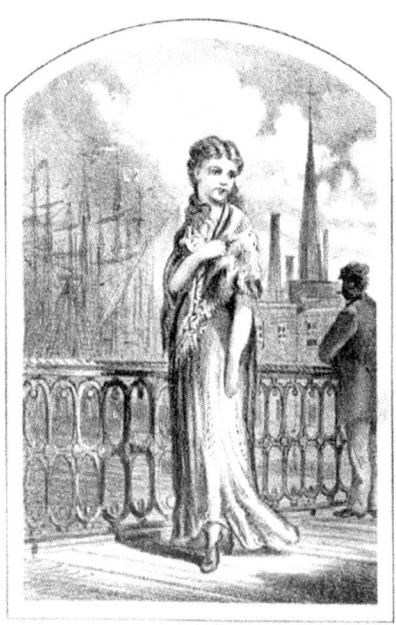

"The Outcast." *From* Police Records and Recollections, *1873.*

of vices," would provide the police with evidence against the houses, but by their charter, their agents were forbidden to enter a known house of ill fame, so the evidence was always secondhand. The police were reluctant to follow up on these cases, and when they did, the district attorney was reluctant to prosecute.

Lizzie Barry had previously been an inmate at 52 Pitts but said she had been thrown out for trying to protect a fifteen-year-old girl named Lizzie Merchant who was being held there against her will. This was a charge that the police could not ignore. In exchange for probation, Miss Barry agreed to leave Boston and return to her home in Worcester, so believing she was safe from retribution by the managers of 52 Pitts, she told the police everything she knew about Lizzie Merchant's captivity.

The officers thoroughly searched the house, calling out for the young girl, but were unable to find her until they opened the door to a darkened garret at the top house and found Lizzie Merchant, stark naked, alone and crying. Seeing Officer Hogan in his uniform, she implored him to take her away. Hogan gathered enough clothing from the other inmates to provide Lizzie an ill-fitting suit and took her back to the station house.

Though her face was pale and haggard and her figure slight and girlish, Lizzie Merchant was strikingly beautiful, with a wealth of nut-brown hair and large hazel eyes. Lizzie had not been outside the garret in three months. She had been seduced and drugged, Lizzie told the police, by someone she thought was her friend. Kept alone in the dark room, she was forced to live a life of shame.

Lizzie's was the kind of story that made national news and reinforced the widespread fear that "white slavers" were preying on innocent young girls in America and selling them into prostitution. The fears were overblown; in fact, most prostitutes were fallen women driven to prostitution as a last resort after being abandoned by their families. But Lizzie Merchant had been so

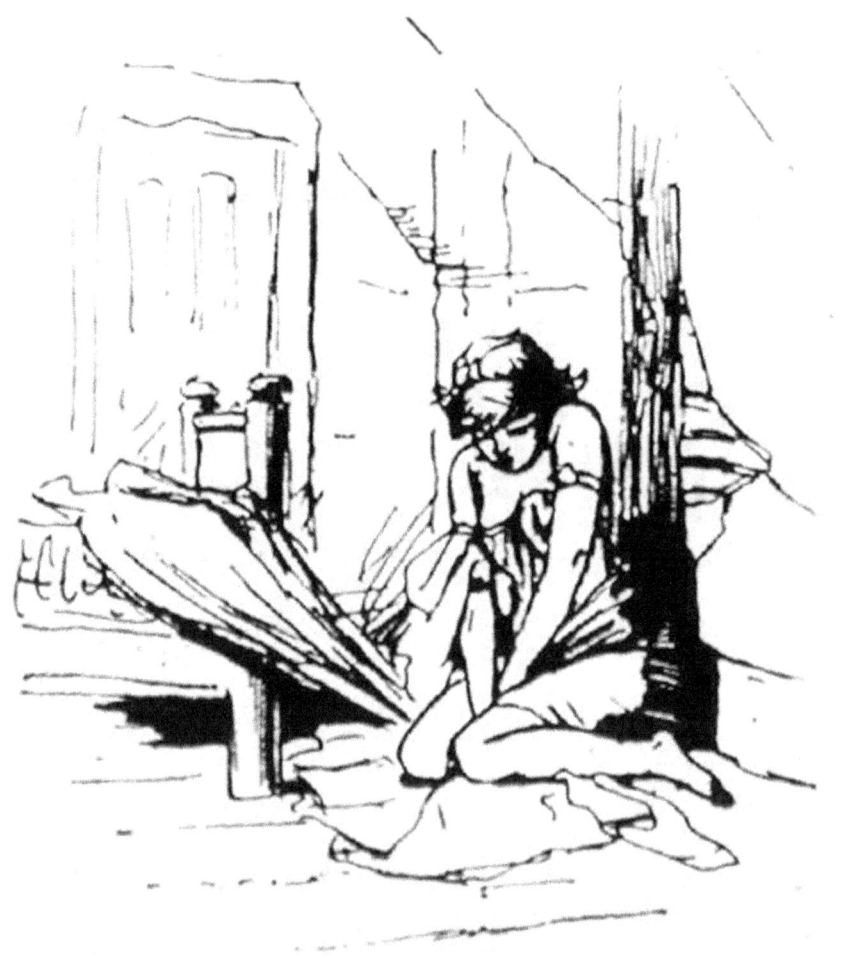

Lizzie Merchant in the garret. *From* National Police Gazette, *November 11, 1885.*

helpless and vulnerable that her entrapment by the demi-monde seemed almost inevitable.

She was born in Nova Scotia, but both parents died when she was only six months old, and Lizzie was sent to live with an aunt in Gloucester, Massachusetts. She was said to be a remarkably handsome child with great natural talents but little opportunity to cultivate them. Her aunt died in 1883, leaving Lizzie on her own at age thirteen. Like so many poor Massachusetts girls, Lizzie moved to Boston to find work. She was young and delicate in constitution, making it difficult to find suitable employment, but Lizzie was determined to avoid the life of dissipation that befell so many young girls who came to the city. Finally, she found a position taking care of the children of a West End family. The family owned a drinking establishment and soon decided that Lizzie was wasted on the children and put her to work in the saloon, first as a dishwasher and then as a barmaid. With her pretty face and innocent bearing, Lizzie attracted much attention at the saloon, including among a group of unscrupulous men who had designs on her.

One warm August night, she met a young man she knew on Green Street. He asked where she was going, and she said she was going to the saloon but had some time before she had to start working.

"Well," he said, "you are in no hurry, come with me for half an hour, and we will go to the museum and see some great curiosities."

He told her all the wonders they would see at the Dime Museum, and Lizzie agreed to go. He took her hand and led her to Pitts Street. Stopping at No. 52, he said he had some friends there that he wanted to ask along. She followed him inside. Lizzie described the scene to the police after her rescue:

We went into a large room, and there I waited for the fellow, while he went out to invite his friend to go with us, as I supposed. Presently several people came in, among them the young man who had invited me to go with him. I told him that we must make haste, as I had got work to do; but he said with a laugh:

"I guess there isn't much need of hurrying. We will stay here a little while;" and then wine was passed around.

I refused to take any at first, but they urged me to it and finally, just to keep them quiet, I drank one little glass, it tasted queer, but I did not know the flavor of wine very well, and so could not tell whether there was anything wrong with it or not. The conversation continued, although I kept saying that I must go. Soon a strange feeling passed over me. I seemed to be getting very sleepy. My companion was not ready to go, and so I thought I would just close my eyes for a second before we should start. I tried not to go to sleep. Gradually, however, the sound of the voices grew less audible, until finally, they ceased altogether.

I remember nothing more that happened until I awoke, and I was in a darkened chamber in company with the fellow who was to have taken me to the museum. Then, for the first time, it came to me that I had been victimized. I was horrified at my situation. After all my efforts to live an honest life, it seemed as if the fates had conspired to work my ruin.

Lizzie was told that she was in a house of ill repute and would not be allowed to leave. The proprietor, Bill Dow, said that she was to live there and pay him twelve dollars a week for board. Of course, there was only one way to earn the required twelve dollars, and Lizzie was forced into a life of shame.

She had tried to escape by breaking open a window blind, but the noise attracted attention, and one of the men of the house rushed in. He beat her with a club until she fainted. Weeks of pain and sickness followed; when it appeared that Lizzie was dying, a doctor was brought in to attend her. Gradually, she regained her health.

The police planned to investigate the case further, and if they pressed charges, Lizzie Merchant would testify at the hearing. Following that, she would be sent to the Dedham Temporary Home for Women and Children. Lizzie Barry would also be called to testify, but when Officer Hogan went looking for her, she could not be found. He suspected that she was being held at 52 Pitts; he called for her there but was told she had gone. The next day, he returned, armed with a search warrant, ostensibly looking for contraband liquor. Behind one locked door, he found Lizzie Barry, who claimed that when she returned to the house for her clothes, the proprietor had brutally beaten her for telling the police about Lizzie Merchant. Hogan arrested the proprietor, Charles Barnard, alias Charles Buzzell, alias Bill Dow.

Both Lizzie Barry and Lizzie Merchant testified against Charles Barnard, and he was found guilty of keeping a house of ill fame at 52 Pitts Street and sentenced to one year in the house of correction. He was also found guilty of unlawfully selling liquor at that address and was fined $100 and costs. Reportedly, Barnard was the proprietor of six different houses of prostitution in the West End and treated all his inmates harshly.

By the end of the 1870s, those who profited most from the social evil were not those who directly operated brothels; it was the owners behind the scenes who, at least nominally, adopted an air of respectability and were shielded from prosecution. A coordinated raid in April 1876 targeted at least five West End brothels, and all of the managers arrested were women. The *Boston Globe* reported that the house at 5 Eaton Place was said to be run by Bose Cobb, though he was not present and was not arrested. The six houses managed by Charles Barnard were actually owned by Thomas Paton, whom the *Globe* called "the king of brothel keepers."

The *Boston City Directory* listed Bose Cobb's occupation as dance hall owner and Thomas Paton's as liquor dealer—not highly regarded professions but not criminal. Reverend Morgan contended that those most responsible for prostitution in Boston were not disreputable men like Cobb or Paton but respectable city leaders who directly or indirectly profited from the use of their property for immoral purposes.

Morgan visited the leading property owners of the city, asking them to sign a pledge not to lease their buildings for immoral purposes. He received much verbal support for the enterprise and even some donations, but very few would sign the pledge. The strongest opposition came from politicians and church officials. Morgan blamed silence in the press and laxity of policemen who were "like perambulating statues, without eyes or ears." It seemed clear that many of the city's leading citizens were leading double lives—righteous and respectable on the surface, while in the background profiting from the vilest of sins. And the city's institutions were happy to keep it that way.

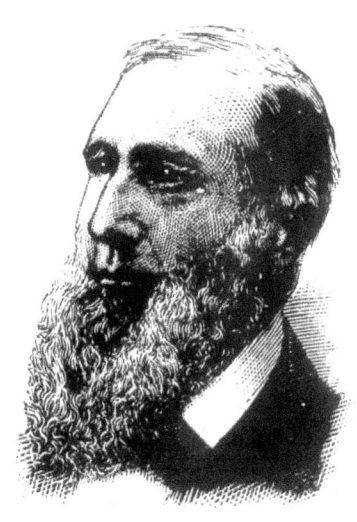

Edward S. Sanborn. *From* National Police Gazette, *October 10, 1885.*

The most extreme example of a brothel keeper living a double life was Edward Sanborn, who owned several houses of ill fame in the West End but was considered an upstanding patron of education and religion in his hometown of Kingston, New Hampshire. Edward Steven Sanborn was born in 1819 to a prominent family in Kingston. He enlisted to fight in the Union army and left the service in 1865 with the rank of major. After the war, Sanborn settled in Boston and, while never cutting ties to his hometown, began a life much different than the one he had known growing up. He became a libertine, frequenting West End brothels, and joined with a group of women to open a brothel of his own, using money inherited from his father.

Sanborn had the reputation of a tough, unscrupulous businessman who "insisted on realizing more for his money than anyone else could get." He was also a notorious miser who would rather walk a mile and a half than pay a horsecar fare. But his frugality paid off—before long, he owned at least three profitable, upscale brothels in the West End.

While living this unseemly life in Boston, Sanborn made regular trips back to Kingston, where he was viewed as a model citizen. He was a

Congregationalist who donated generously to his church but also gave freely to the Universalists and Methodists. In Kingston, he was a great believer in churches, saying, "They are necessary to keep the boys and girls out of deviltry." Though he spent more time in Boston, Sanborn was so well liked in Kingston that the people elected him as their representative to the state legislature.

Around 1868, at age forty-nine, Sanborn met Miss Julia A. Hilton, a pretty nineteen-year-old girl who had come to Boston from Maine, and they began a seventeen-year relationship that lasted until Julia's death. They lived together at his residence in a brothel he kept on Lyman Street. To the world, she was his housekeeper, but in fact, she was his mistress and the manager of the Lyman Street house. Sanborn made Julia an equal partner in all of his business ventures, and she proved to possess the same business acumen as her lover, amassing a small fortune of her own. Beyond their business partnership, though they never married, it was clear that their relationship was deep and loving.

The couple never had children, and in his sixties, Sanborn began to concern himself with his legacy and the disposition of his estate. He had a monument erected in a Kingston cemetery where he and Julia Hilton were to be buried side by side. At the time, he was peeved with Kingston for not reelecting him to the legislature, so he left the town nothing in his will. Instead, he left $40,000 to Dartmouth College and the remainder to his sisters and to the son of ex-Governor Noyes of Ohio (the governor had been a classmate many years earlier).

Sanborn soon had a change of heart. He learned that his relatives had been criticizing him behind his back, and he struck them from the will. He had second thoughts regarding his bequest to Dartmouth; he realized that the memory of his gift would last only as long as it took to cash the check. He removed Dartmouth from his will and set out instead to build and endow an elegant brick and granite school building in Kingston, to be called the Sanborn Seminary. It was to be a non-sectarian institution for the education of the youth of both sexes. Julia Hilton would personally fund the school's library. Life-size marble busts of both donors would be displayed over a plaque reading: "This seminary was founded and endowed and this building erected by Edward Stevens Sanborn in token of his regard for his native town and his appreciation of the importance of education. The library was presented by Julia Ann Hilton."

Sanborn's new will left $5,000 to the Congregational Church of Kingston, $1,000 to Mrs. George W. Sanborn, a $250 annuity to Mary E. Brickett of

Haverhill and the income of $2,000 to the poor women of Kingston, "whom the selectmen may adjudge best entitled to the benefit by their industry and virtue." The remainder, over $200,000, would go to the Sanborn Seminary.

At the same time the Sanborn Seminary was being built in Kingston, Edward Sanborn was also building a new brothel in Boston, which he envisioned as the most glorious house of prostitution in the country. All work in Boston came to a halt in April 1885 with the sudden death of Julia Hilton. In her will, Julia left the bulk of her fortune, over $80,000, to Edward Sanborn, but Sanborn cared nothing for the money; he had lost the love of his life. He took sick shortly after her death and never fully recovered. Sanborn died that September.

The story of Edward Sanborn's double life would probably have remained a secret, but a contentious legal battle over his and Julia's wills made national headlines. Sanborn's disinherited relatives, who in the penultimate will would have inherited the bulk of his estate, contended that he was not in his right mind when he drafted the new will and wanted it nullified. Although the president of Dartmouth College, Congregational minister Reverend Samuel C. Bartlett, was also a vice-president of the New England Society for the Suppression of Vice, the college joined Sanborn's relatives in the fight for the brothel keeper's fortune. To complicate matters, Julia Hilton's relatives were contesting her will, claiming that Edward

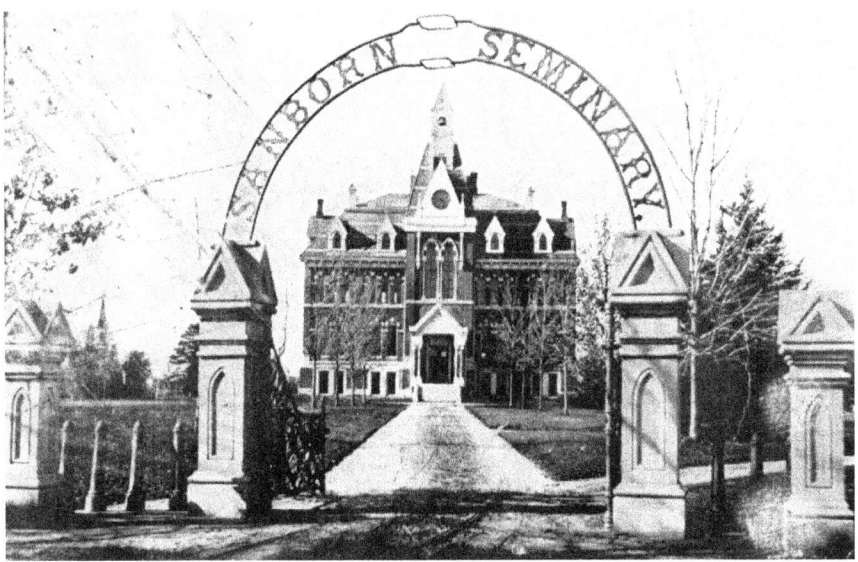

Sanborn Seminary, postcard. *Author's collection.*

Sanborn had undue influence over her, so it was not clear exactly how much would be in Sanborn's estate. Meanwhile, the Sanborn Seminary had been completed but lacked the funding necessary to open and operate; the trustees could do little but wait for the outcome of the cases.

Newspapers across the country loved the story of Sanborn's double life and his romantic attachment to a woman thirty years his junior, but they had no sympathy for the man himself. They called him a "monster of depravity," "degraded miser" and "moral leper," and regarding Boston, it was "a most remarkable story of the immorality of the city of culture."

The plaintiffs in both cases joined forces and succeeded in moving the trials from Massachusetts to New Hampshire, where they thought they had a better chance of winning. In the end, however, there was very little evidence that Sanborn had been of unsound mind or had undue influence over Julia Hilton. In both cases, the court upheld the final will, and Sanborn Seminary received the bulk of both estates.

Sanborn Seminary opened in 1888 and educated New Hampshire children as a private institution for the next seventy-eight years. Its success overshadowed the tawdry battle of two Yankee families and a college with ties to the Congregational Church over possession of Boston whorehouse profits.

Chapter 7

CONFIDENCE

*C*harles Francis Adams was the son of President John Quincy Adams, grandson of President John Adams and a statesman in his own right, having served as a United States congressman and as President Lincoln's ambassador to the Court of St. James's. In 1882, at age seventy-six, Adams had retired from public life and was living quietly in his home on Beacon Hill. While taking a stroll one morning that March, a young man hailed Adams and introduced himself as J.S. Morrison, son of an old friend. Though C.F. Adams had a reputation for being cold and somewhat antisocial, he took an instant liking to this personable and intelligent young man. Morrison had a boyish look, with red hair and freckles, but was impeccably dressed and had the bearing of a gentleman. When he asked to join Adams on his morning walk, the old man agreed without hesitation.

In their conversation, the young man made references to speeches Adams had made and quoted lines from memory, but as they turned onto Boylston Street, he abruptly changed the subject. He told Adams that he was holding a winning ticket in the Havana Lottery and asked if Adams would accompany him as he went in to the lottery office at 31 Boylston to claim his prize. Adams agreed, and both men went in. The lottery office was clean and businesslike, giving the impression of a bank—this was a gross deception. The young man was not the son of an old friend but a New York City confidence man named Jimmy "The Kid" Fitzgerald, and he had no intention of letting Charles Adams leave the office without leaving behind a large sum of money.

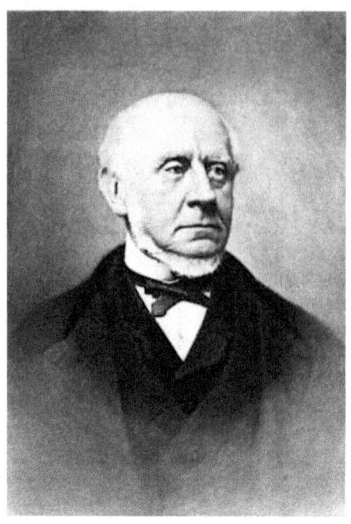

Charles Francis Adams. *Wikimedia Commons.*

Boston was a favorite setting for confidence men throughout the Victorian era. As a center of commerce and a busy seaport, the city was a confluence of business travelers, countrymen selling their crops and sailors on leave—all carrying dangerous amounts of cash. Local citizens, prosperous and a little too trusting, made good marks as well.

The Society for the Suppression of Vice, whose scope was broad but not always deep, included in its 1885 and 1886 annual reports a warning to women to avoid a fraud being advertised in local newspapers. A company was offering, for one dollar, a book of instructions enabling any woman to create artwork, which, if satisfactory, would be liberally paid for by the company. Of course, the work was never satisfactory, and the women lost their dreams and their dollars. As insidious as it was, this scam was tiny compared to the con games regularly practiced in Boston.

Military procurement has always provided a good cover for confidence men, and Boston, with its manufacturing and shipping interests, became a prime target. The most audacious swindler working before the Civil War was Chauncey Larkin, who wore an army uniform and took various aliases, such as Colonel Gorman, Colonel DuPont, Colonel Dudley and Lieutenant Smith. In Boston, he was known as Lieutenant Hunter. Posing as a purchaser for the army, he put together large deals for real estate, ships, merchandise, coal and produce. The sellers were so dazzled by the size of the deal that they had no objection to paying the buyer a small kickback in advance. Of course, Larkin never took delivery of the goods and could never be found to collect payment.

The exploits of "Lieutenant Hunter" became legendary in the Boston Police Department. One story involved a local hotel that, at considerable expense, had just furnished a suite of rooms as bridal chambers, calculated to become the pride of the establishment. Lieutenant Hunter learned of this and decided that he should christen the rooms himself, so the dashing lieutenant and his "wife" jumped into a hack and proceeded to the hotel. He told the desk clerk that he and his lady had just been married in Providence, Rhode

Island. The couple's baggage and their servants, he said, had apparently gotten lost en route, no doubt proceeding to the wrong hotel. He would deal with that in the morning, he said, and then persuaded the clerk to give them the new bridal suite. The joyous newlyweds sat down to an extravagant dinner and then retired to their splendidly furnished chambers. The manager let the couple sleep late the next day, but when he finally knocked on the door, he got no response; they had checked out early, leaving behind a large unpaid bill.

Chauncey Larkin did not remain at large for long; he was arrested for swindling a merchant at one of the wharves out of $300. He was convicted

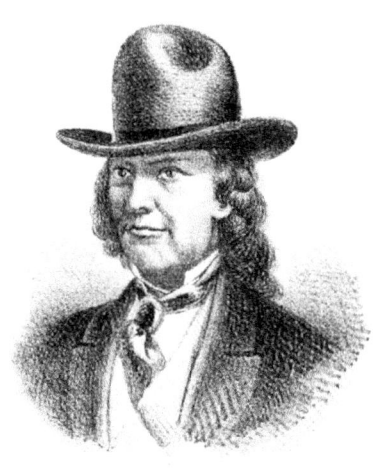

"Confidence Man." *From* Police Records and Recollections, *1873.*

and sentenced to the State Prison at Charlestown for three years. Upon his release, Larkin continued his regular career around the country. He was arrested again in Boston in 1862 and on April 1 was extradited to New York on an open warrant there. As he departed for New York and a probable stay at Sing Sing Prison, he took a very gentlemanly leave of those in the office and remarked, "This is All-Fool's day, and I am a large stockholder."

At the street level, grifters ran short-con games at railroad stations and hotels. Newspapers warned of a con man named "English Jim" selling worthless rings at a premium, enticing buyers by implying that they were stolen. William Baker sold counterfeit bonds by the wharves, with a hard-luck story about needing fast cash to travel. He sold the bonds at half the face value, promising to buy them back, with interest, upon his return. Of course, he never returned to reclaim the worthless bonds.

The classic "shell game" and its variations, "thimblerig" and "three-card monte," have always been popular in Boston, in spite of being revealed as fraud countless times. "It seems as if every successive generation of men," wrote Benjamin P. Eldridge, Boston superintendent of police, in 1896, "was blindly or stubbornly bent upon burning its fingers in the same old ways in spite of rows of burnt fingers that stretch back through the centuries into time immemorial."

Another classic swindle that proved continually successful, despite the widespread publication of its fraudulent nature, was the "gold brick game." It was already old hat in 1882 when "a gentleman of means" (name withheld) responded to this advertisement in a Boston newspaper: "Wanted—A partner. To any person having $1000 at immediate command I will confide the details of a business operation that will realize a profit of at least $10,000 within a month: loss impossible, as money will be fully secured and investing parties will have full control."

The gentleman responded by mail and some time later received a visit at his place of business from Joseph Eaton, the man who had placed the ad. Eaton told the gentleman that he had just returned from California; he had stolen some property and was compelled to leave the state. The property in question included a fair number of solid gold bricks. He had one brick in his possession and needed money to enable his partner to return to California and secure the remaining bricks. For $1,000, the gentleman would take possession of a gold brick worth ten times that amount, with an option to buy even more. The gentleman expressed interest and arranged to meet with Eaton at Porter's Hotel in Cambridge to see the brick.

At the hotel, Eaton showed the gentleman an impressive-looking brick of gold. To prove it was solid, Eaton bored into the brick with an auger; he gave the scrapings to the gentleman and advised him to have them analyzed to prove it was real gold. He took the scrapings to a chemist, who affirmed that they were pure gold. The gentleman was convinced, but the "gold brick" Eaton had shown him was actually a gold-plated brick of lead. One small section of the brick had been dug out and replaced with real gold, and that was where he applied the auger.

While anxious to conclude the deal, the gentleman did not wish to enter any bargain without the advice of his counsel, so he brought his attorney to the next meeting with Eaton. The attorney, who should have seen through the scam right away, was first as convinced as his client and advised him to go ahead with the deal. As negotiations continued over how much the gentleman would invest, the attorney began to suspect the deal was a fraud and took the story to the police.

The police saw right away that it was the classic gold brick game and convinced the gentleman to participate in a sting operation. The following Saturday, when a meeting was scheduled to consummate the deal, the police would be waiting to catch the con man red-handed. That morning, the gentleman grew anxious about meeting with a man he now knew was a thief and went first to city hall to make sure the police were ready to follow through. But Eaton and his confederates had been watching the gentleman, and Eaton, realizing that he was being set up by the police, did not show up for the meeting.

Joseph Eaton was arrested soon after for attempting a gold brick swindle, but without evidence, the police had no grounds to hold him. He was photographed at the police station and then put on a train to New York City and instructed never again to return to Boston.

As elaborate as the gold brick swindle was, it was still a small-time operation compared to what Jimmy Fitzgerald had planned for Charles Francis Adams. Landing a big fish like Adams took organization and finesse, and Fitzgerald was prepared. After paying the lottery prize, the cashier, who was actually Fitzgerald's partner, Johnny Norton, told him that he was also entitled to a chance of increasing his winnings in a special drawing—the game of banco. This was the real reason Fitzgerald had brought Adams to the office.

Banco was a gambling game in the same way that three-card monte is a gambling game; the mark believes he has a chance to win, but the outcome is always predetermined. The term would later evolve into "bunco" and be used in reference to any fraudulent game. In its simplest form, the original game of banco consists of a cloth layout with numbered flaps. The player rolls dice or draws a numbered card to determine which flap is revealed. If the flap is covering a prize amount, that amount is added to his winnings; if it is covering a star, he wins no prize for that turn. At least one flap is designated as a "conditional," where the player must pay an amount set by the banker or forfeit all of his winnings. Another flap called the "state number" covers a blank space. If the player draws the state number before the last roll, the game ends and the player loses everything. Invariably, the player will win increasing amounts followed by conditionals until he has a sizeable amount invested, and then he will roll the state number and lose it all. This scheme has endless variations, with additional rules to make the game more complicated and keep the mark confused.

Fitzgerald agreed to join the game and talked Adams into joining as well. Adams let his new friend roll the dice for both of them. He watched as the young man rolled and won them each a prize of $2,500. In this version of the game, Adams was required to pay 10 percent to continue, and Morrison convinced him that writing a check for $250 was a sound investment. As the game progressed, Adams wrote two more checks—one for $1,200 and one for an astounding $17,500. The office had blank checks on hand from the appropriate bank. Someone else filled in the numbers and made them out to the bearer, but Adams then signed both sides of each check. Of course, the last roll was the state number, and Adams lost it all.

The cashier told Adams in no uncertain terms that he had lost the game, and he must honor his checks. Adams began weeping. He had never gambled before; what would his sons say? Fitzgerald feigned tears as well, saying that he was ruined. He walked the old man home but stayed outside watching until he was certain that Adams would not go to the police.

Banco steerers worked in pairs; the "feeler" gathered as much information as he could about the mark, and the "catcher" used the information to gain the mark's confidence and rope him in. Though most of the information about Charles Francis Adams was public knowledge, Fitzgerald's feeler, Johnny Norton, had ties to Boston's business community and probably supplied the information about his bank and the size of his account (Adams usually carried a balance of $20,000; they hit him for $19,250).

Norton and Fitzgerald had worked together in New York City, where several years earlier the pair had been arrested after taking railroad tycoon Jay Gould for $4,000, and although Gould did not press charges, both men were photographed for New York Police inspector Thomas Byrne's "Rogues' Gallery" of professional criminals. The Boston Police knew that Fitzgerald and Norton were in town but up to this point were satisfied that they were not engaged in any dishonest business. Norton had opened a real estate office in Pemberton Square, and Fitzgerald, though not so enterprising, had given the police no cause for suspicion.

Norton deposited the $17,500 check through his lawyer; he would withdraw the cash as soon as the check cleared. On April 3, a private detective named Benjamin Heath visited Johnny Norton at his office and told him that Mr. Adams's balance was not sufficient to cover the check and Mr. Adams's attorney wanted to discuss the matter. He persuaded Norton to accompany him to the law office of Richard Olney (who would later serve as both attorney general and secretary of state under President Grover Cleveland). Though Charles Francis Adams himself had not yet been notified, his son, John Quincy Adams II, was present in Olney's office when Johnny Norton arrived.

Norton told them that he had no direct connection to the check, saying that he had helped his friend J.S. Morrison cash it because Morrison had promised to repay a debt with the proceeds. Morrison told him he had won the money from Adams; the check was payment for a gambling loss. Olney called him a liar; Adams had never gambled in his life. Norton again denied any knowledge of the affair and suggested that they bring in Morrison and ask him. This was not Norton turning on his partner; it was the next stage of their scam.

They sent word to Fitzgerald, who was still using the name J.S. Morrison, and he agreed to come in and talk after receiving assurance that he would not be arrested on the way to Olney's office, during the meeting or on the way home. Fitzgerald arrived at Olney's office and came right to the point.

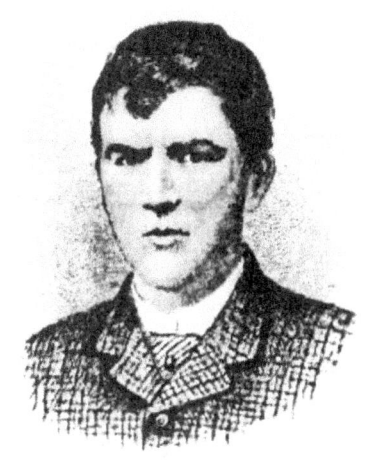

James Fitzgerald. *From* Defenders and Offenders, *1888.*

"Gentlemen, this is my business. My occupation is to allure elderly gentlemen of wealth into some den and extort money from them."

Fitzgerald proceeded to explain how he had gained Mr. Adams's confidence and induced him to enter the office on Boylston Street. He described the game of banco and related the series of events that led Adams to write checks of increasing amounts without really knowing what was going on. Someone in the room asked whether the game was fraudulent, to which Fitzgerald replied, "Oh, yes, it was all a fraud, for that matter."

Olney expressed disbelief that Fitzgerald would be able to deceive Mr. Adams this way.

"You think yourself a pretty smart man, Mr. Olney, but I can rope you in," Fitzgerald replied. "Not now probably, but if I had tried it before you became acquainted with the case. I have roped in smarter men than either you or Mr. Adams. That is my business, and I can do it again."

Though sometimes there was a struggle, he explained, in the end, his victims always paid the checks to protect their reputations. Fitzgerald was confident that Mr. Adams would do the same.

The men in Olney's office kept their word and did not have Fitzgerald arrested then. The Adams family deliberated and concluded that the damage to the reputation of Charles Francis Adams would not be great enough to justify the loss of nearly $20,000; they decided instead to press charges. The con men must have gotten wind of their decision because that evening Fitzgerald and Norton left Boston on separate trains. Fitzgerald, who had been under surveillance, was arrested on board the train; Norton managed to elude capture.

With the arrest came the inevitable publicity. The family was forced to publicly admit that the mind of Charles Francis Adams had been gradually failing. Not all of the press coverage was sympathetic; some editorials expressed the opinion that Adams should be held accountable for his debts. But what fascinated the press was the identity of the perpetrator. The police knew right away that they had Jimmy Fitzgerald in custody, and every newspaper had its own story about "The Kid." Though Inspector Byrnes said Fitzgerald was from Washington, D.C., the *New York Herald-Tribune* said he was born in New York and had a Harvard education. The *Boston Herald* said he was from Hyde Park, Illinois. Others said Fitzgerald was from Milwaukee and had left a government appointment for a life of crime. Jimmy Fitzgerald seemed to have quite a résumé for a man not yet twenty-six years old.

That June, James Fitzgerald was tried and convicted of larceny and sentenced to five years in Charlestown prison. Though Johnny Norton escaped punishment, his freedom did not last long. He died of consumption in New York City in 1885. Charles Francis Adams also did not live to see his assailant released from jail. In November 1886, he died of old age at his Mount Vernon Street home in Boston. It is unclear what became of Jimmy Fitzgerald upon his release from Charlestown, but it is likely that he returned to his stated profession, banco steering. If so, he kept to shallower waters thereafter and avoided headline-grabbing crimes such as scamming a president's son.

Chapter 8

FRESH FROM THE BOGS

On November 3, 1851, Boston's first Irish policeman introduced himself to his fellow officers as "Barney McGinniskin, fresh from the bogs of Ireland." He was not, in fact, "fresh from the bogs"; he had been living in Boston twenty-two years. McGinniskin was trying to make light of the controversy surrounding his appointment. In political circles, an Irishman on the public payroll was no laughing matter. Anti-Irish prejudice had been building in the 1840s as waves of immigrants arrived in Boston escaping the potato famine in Ireland, and many native-born Bostonians felt the city was under siege.

Most members of Boston's police force (238 men in 1855) were not born in Boston; about two-thirds came from out of state, mostly northern New England. They were farm boys who had come to the city to seek their fortune, and many had worked as apprentices or independent teamsters and drivers. Whenever a position opened on the force, dozens would apply. The police force provided steady work, paying about twice what a laborer made with plenty of opportunities for unreported income.

For the growing ranks of Irish immigrants in Boston, finding work of any kind was a problem. Prejudice against hiring the newcomers was so strong that newspaper want ads often bore the tagline, "No Irish need apply" or sometimes just the abbreviation "NINA," leaving Irish workers to compete for only the most menial construction and mill jobs. Irish immigrants were barred from public employment over fears that, as Catholics, they owed their allegiance to a "foreign prince" in Rome.

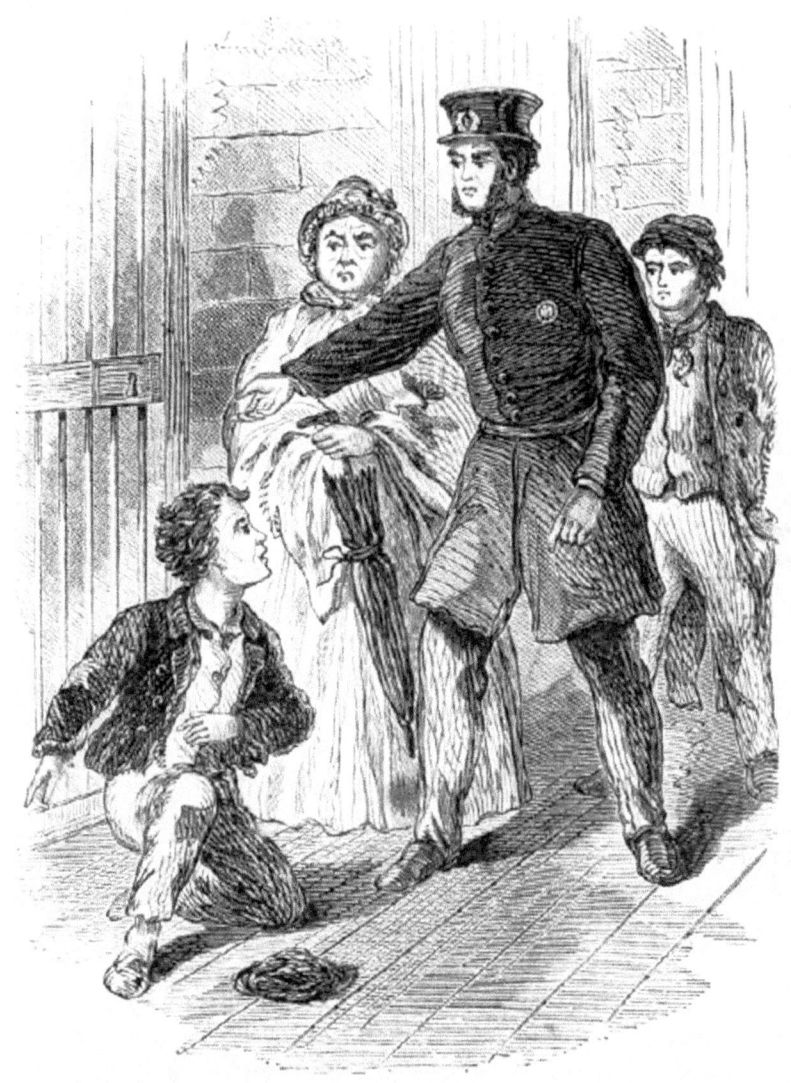

A Boston policeman. *From* Ned Nevins the Newsboy, *1867.*

Anti-Catholic prejudice had been part of Boston's culture since the days of the Puritans. Popery was high on the list of sins that drove the Puritans to the New World, and tolerance was not among their virtues. In 1688, Ann Glover, an indentured servant born in Ireland, was seen praying the

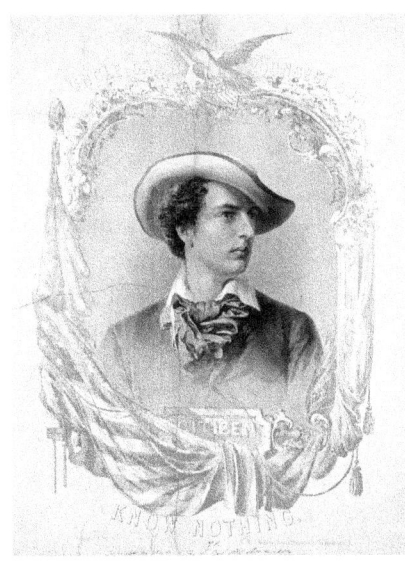

"Citizen Know-Nothing." *Wikimedia Commons.*

rosary and was accused of witchcraft. She was sentenced to death because at her trial she would not, or could not, recite the Lord's Prayer in English, saying it instead in Gaelic and Latin. In 1834, 146 years later, anti-Catholic sentiment was still alive; fear and superstition led an angry mob to burn down the Ursuline Convent in Charlestown.

In the 1840s, as Irish immigrants were arriving in Boston in unprecedented numbers, the prejudice took the form of the anti-immigrant American Party. Better known as the Know-Nothings, they modeled their movement after the Freemasons, meeting in secret with oaths and initiation rituals, and when questioned by outsiders, members would claim to "know nothing." Their membership was limited to native-born, Protestant men.

Formed as an anti-establishment party, the Know-Nothings opposed not just immigrants and their supporters in the Democratic Party but the patrician Whigs as well, whom they called "party hacks," "wire-pullers," "money bags" and "kid-gloved gentry." The Know-Nothings were not a top-down hierarchy like the Whigs and Democrats but proved to be effective grassroots organizers, drawing their candidates from within local lodges.

The Know-Nothings were also antislavery, in opposition to the Democrats who owed their national strength to southern slaveholders and who frightened their immigrant constituents in the north with the specter of freed slaves taking their jobs. The Know-Nothings' antislavery position attracted abolitionists, who had also become disaffected with the Whigs and were willing to accept the Know-Nothings' bigotry on immigration to further the greater cause of abolishing slavery. The party also attracted those in the temperance movement who saw the Democrats as controlled by the "rum interests" but received little support from the Whig establishment.

Both major parties denounced the brand of "dark-lantern" politics practiced by the Know-Nothings, but neither party took them seriously until the Massachusetts election of 1854, when the American Party received the largest number of votes of any party to that time. When the votes were counted, Boston had a Know-Nothing mayor, Massachusetts had a Know-Nothing governor and the Know-Nothings had won virtually every elective office in the state.

Once in power, the Know-Nothing governor, Henry J. Gardner, took steps to "Americanize America," pushing nativists' concerns ahead of all others with proposals such as a literacy test and a twenty-one-year residency requirement as prerequisites to voting and limiting public office to native-born citizens. They feared that if Irish immigrants could vote and hold office, they would unite and form a corrupt political machine like New York's Tammany Hall. But little of the Know-Nothings' agenda was accomplished, and their coalition soon broke down as the new leaders became the new elites, as self-serving as the Whigs and Democrats, and the American Party lost its grassroots support. As effective as they had been in 1854, the Know-Nothings had no second act, and in 1857, the support they had once enjoyed went to the nascent Republican Party.

Extreme anti-Irish sentiment among native-born Bostonians, for the most part, ended with the Civil War. After fighting side by side with Irish Americans through that terrible conflict to preserve the Union, it was hard to picture them owing greater allegiance to the pope of Rome. Only the most rabid anti-Catholics, like Reverend Henry Morgan, continued the fight.

But in Barney McGinniskin's day, anti-Irish sentiment was still strong. City Marshal Francis Tukey took a bold step in 1851 by appointing McGinniskin to the police force, but in 1854, with the Know-Nothings in power, Tukey reversed himself and dismissed Barney McGinniskin for no other reason than being Irish.

Alderman Abel B. Monroe considered an Irish policeman to be a "dangerous precedent" because "Irishmen commit most of the city's crime and would receive special consideration from any of their own wearing blue." While there was no reason to think Barney McGinniskin would be any more corrupt than the rest of the force, Alderman Monroe was not wrong in his assessment of the Irish contribution to crime in Boston. By 1850, two-thirds of Boston's saloons were Irish-owned, and whiskey was cheap. Incidents of drunkenness and violent crime had risen in direct proportion to the city's growing Irish population.

While crime, in most cases, was an unfortunate consequence of the extreme poverty and underemployment faced by Irish immigrants, the new population of Boston also included some particularly fierce professional criminals. A South End saloon known as the Bag of Worms was one of the most notorious resorts in the city. Unlike the free-and-easies such as Bose Cobb's, no one went to the Bag of Worms looking for a good time. It was the meeting place of the Albany Street Gang, the lowest brand of sneak thieves and highwaymen who would gather after making a haul to divvy up the loot and celebrate their score. The undisputed leader of this gang was a young South Boston man of Irish extraction named Edward Welch—better known as "Chicken" Welch or just "The Chicken."

"Chicken" Welch had frequent run-ins with the law but was seldom behind bars. In April 1879, he pleaded guilty to assault and battery and was released on probation. The same year, he was arrested for using profane and vulgar language and for assault and battery for throwing a stone into a passing horsecar. He was fined five dollars for each offense. Welch had an altercation with a man named Sullivan on Broadway in South Boston in 1881, and the police were called when the disagreement escalated into a knife fight. Chicken Welch severed one of Sullivan's fingers, but no arrests were made because Sullivan did not wish to press charges.

Members of the Albany Street Gang managed to avoid prison until 1882, when Welch was convicted of two counts of highway robbery. Edward H. "Chicken" Welch, age twenty-two, was sentenced to ten years in the state prison in Charlestown. Police raided the Bag of Worms and recovered a great quantity of stolen goods. The saloon closed, and the gang broke up.

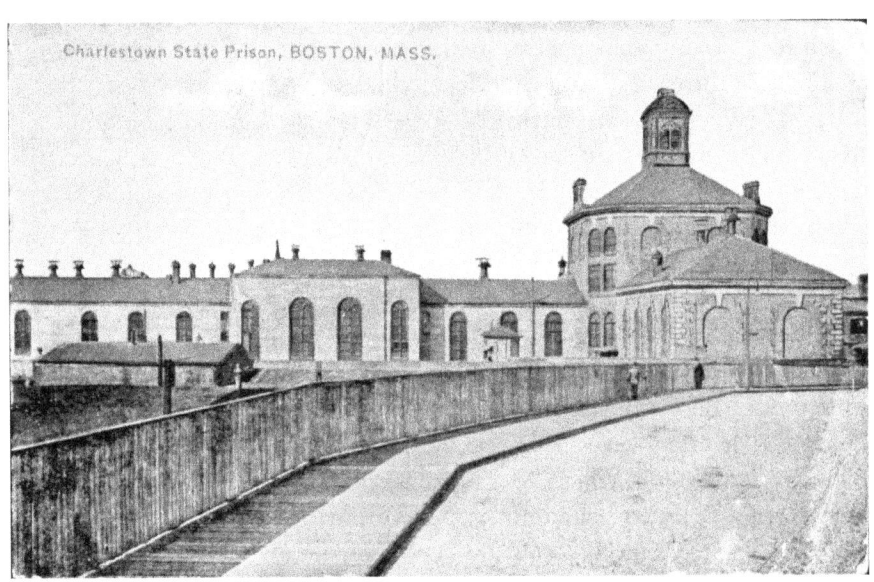

Charlestown Prison, postcard. *Author's collection.*

About two and a half years into his sentence, Chicken Welch and three other prisoners escaped from Charlestown. They had been working on a construction detail in the prison and discovered a loose brick in the ceiling. Around 9:00 a.m. on April 18, 1885, they quickly removed the loose brick and climbed outside. They used a rope to reach the ground and then scaled the walls and fled in four different directions. Welch was at large for six days before Police Sergeant Libby traced him through acquaintances to a building in Roxbury. Libby waited until 2:00 a.m. and then went in with two officers and recaptured him. The jailbreak added three more years to Welch's sentence.

Welch tried to escape at least twice more, including one incident when incarcerated members of the Albany Street Gang incited a riot by shouting and yelling at a predetermined time. One of the prisoners had a revolver and two cartridges. The guards feared for their lives, but the shots missed, and one hundred police officers arrived to quell the riot before anyone could escape.

Chicken Welch was pardoned by Governor Russel in March 1892. The early release was not for good behavior on Welch's part but due to a technicality. Welch saw other prisoners involved in jailbreaks leaving prison after only one extra year and complained that he had been given three extra years. An investigation found that the clerk had written down the maximum sentence when the judge had intended the minimum sentence, one year. Welch had already served most of his original sentence, and the governor decided that the easiest action was just to let him go.

Upon leaving prison, Welch told the warden he had all he wanted of prison life and meant to live straight thereafter, but in 1894, he was in trouble with the law again. He and two of his associates beat and kicked Frank McDermott, sending him to the hospital. He managed to escape prison on this charge, but six months later, he was sentenced to three months in the house of correction for assault and battery for throwing a tumbler at Cornelius Coakley in a South Boston saloon. After his release, Chicken Welch was arrested again for fighting with John Crowley, who lived in the same house. The fight spilled out into the street, and the two men's wives joined in. Crowley was knocked down and left with a broken arm. The following December, Welch was arrested once more when he assaulted Thomas McCarthy with a hammer after McCarthy tried to break up a fight between Welch's dog and another.

Though he never again served any major prison time, Chicken Welch continued to have frequent run-ins with the law. By the end of the century, though, the officers who brought him in were almost certainly fellow Irishmen. The political climate in Boston had changed drastically as Irish politicians rose to power. Barney McGinniskin had been vindicated; the Irish dominated the Boston Police force.

Chapter 9

CHINATOWN

A stranger walking down Harrison Avenue toward the South End in 1886 would find himself suddenly immersed in the sights and sounds of a bustling Asian city. Crossing Essex Street, he would be surrounded by shops and restaurants of Boston's Chinatown with signs in unreadable characters interspersed with anglicized merchant names—Hong Far Low Restaurant, Sam Sing Groceries, Wing Gone, Chong & Co. Importers. Sacks of rice were piled along the wall of the grocery, with displays of herbs and vegetables; from the back of the store, the cackle of chickens could be heard. Men in long shirts and cotton trousers hustled by or idled on street corners, some with long braided queues of hair trailing from tight silk hats. They spoke rudimentary English when required for transactions, but to one another, they spoke a language completely bewildering to western ears, as if they had never left their native land and the white stranger was a foreigner in their midst.

Chinese immigrants began arriving in New England in the 1840s, around the same time as the Irish but in far smaller numbers. Unlike the Irish, the Chinese had little interest in becoming part of the larger community, preferring to remain isolated, tending to their own interests. In Boston, they settled in a small, densely populated stretch of Harrison Avenue and its side streets, which soon became known as Chinatown, and as much as possible, they made it resemble their native land. Here they practiced their traditional customs of diet, religion, justice and social hierarchy, with no regard to western notions.

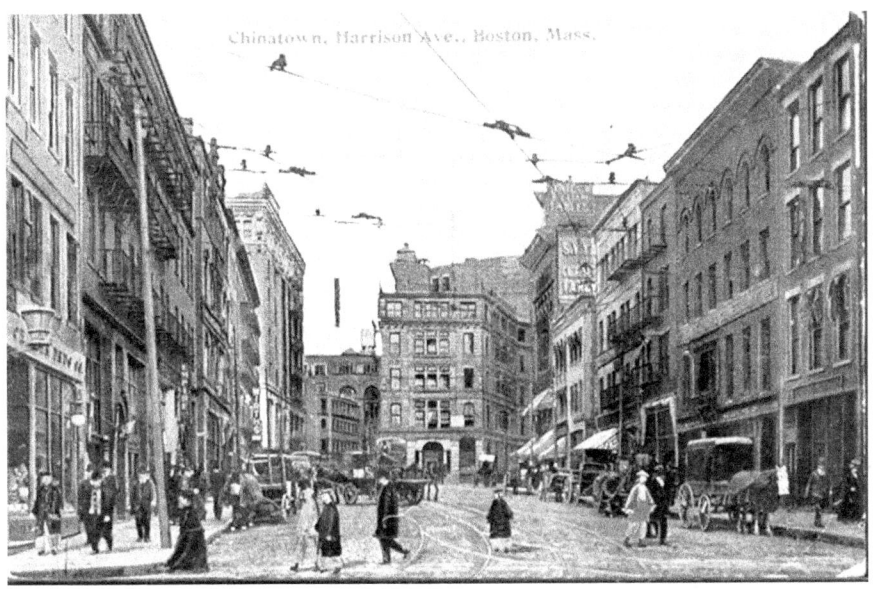

Chinatown, postcard. *Author's collection.*

They also indulged in their traditional vices. When the sun went down on Harrison Avenue, the backrooms and upper floors of the commercial buildings became busy gambling halls and opium joints. At 32 Harrison, gambling was carried on almost incessantly. The Boston Police were aware of what went on in Chinatown, but as in all other parts of the city, they could not raid gamblers unless they had a formal complaint. Throughout the nineteenth century, opium was legal in Massachusetts, though legal importation was tightly regulated and most of Boston's opium was smuggled contraband. But smuggling was a federal crime, and the Boston Police had little interest in the opium trade other than keeping a watchful eye on those who indulged in a habit condemned by nearly everyone outside Chinatown.

Managers of the opium joints in Chinatown were especially aware of the stigma the rest of the city placed on the opium habit and for the most part limited their clientele to fellow countrymen. One large operation on Harrison Avenue had private rooms on the third floor available to white businessmen and politicians, people "who have reputations to lose." Sam Lung ran a joint in a storefront labeled "F. Hayden Roofer" on Orange Street, on the fringes of Chinatown, which catered to white prostitutes. But most white opium smokers went to Chinese-run joints in other parts of the

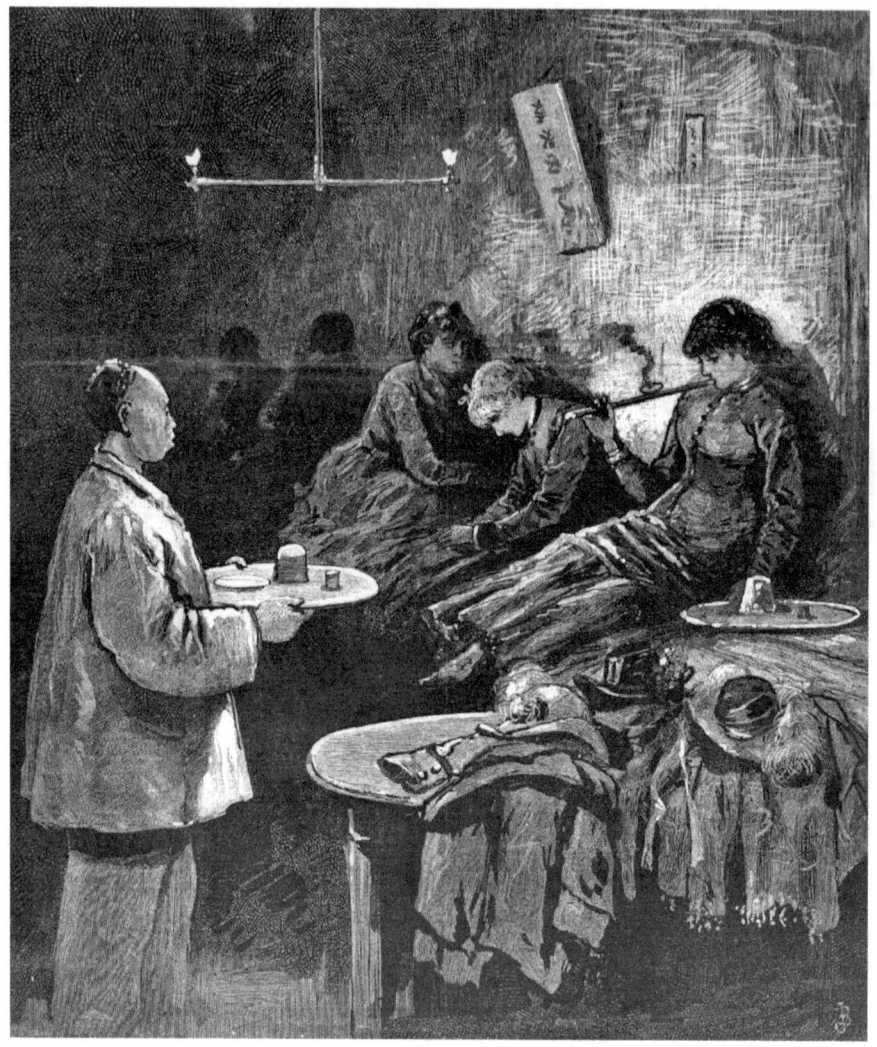

An opium joint. *From* Frank Leslie's Illustrated Newspaper, *May 12, 1883.*

city, such as Quang Sang Long's tea store and laundry on Tremont in the South End and Hop Yuen's laundry on Howard Street in the West End.

Nationwide, the issue of Chinese immigration had become a hot issue. On the West Coast, charges that Chinese workers were depressing wages led to rioting and violence between white and Chinese workers. In 1882, President Arthur signed the Chinese Exclusion Act, prohibiting Chinese immigration to the United States for the next ten years. But in Boston, the controversy was somewhat academic; what was happening in the West had little in common with the Chinese in Boston, and Boston's Chinatown thrived almost unnoticed.

Most Bostonians had little contact with the Chinese, though some adventurous diners visited Chinatown for the food. Hong Far Low, "the first man in Boston to make chop suey," opened a restaurant on Harrison Avenue in 1879 that became a Chinatown landmark lasting well into the twentieth century. The most common interactions between native Bostonians and Chinese immigrants were in the Chinese-run laundries operating throughout the city. The storefront laundries also served as residences for the laundrymen and were divided into three rooms: customers were received in the front, the manager and sometimes an assistant would sleep in the middle room and in the back room a big coke-burning stove boiled water to wash the clothes and gave off the heat to dry them. The laundrymen cooked their meals on the same stove, and at night the back room was used for opium smoking. Customers found the aroma of Chinese laundries pungent and exotic, but they were pleased with the quality and value of the laundry service.

Many of the laundries throughout Boston, as well as the gambling and opium operations in Chinatown, were controlled by mutual protection organizations called "companies." In other parts of the country, they were known as tongs or "hatchet societies." They provided capital and services to advance the members' business interests, as well as providing protection and meting out justice in the community and arranging for lawyers for matters in the outside world. In return, they expected loyalty, obedience and regular payments. Four companies controlled business in Boston's Chinatown: Moy, Ching, Lee and Sing. They were extremely competitive, and relations among them were often "at swords' points."

The most powerful company was Moy, headed by Ah Moy Chong, a notorious gambler who ran a gambling room at 32 Harrison. He was married to a white woman and had a large home on Orange Street. Ah Moy Chong wore a black slouch hat but otherwise dressed in Chinese style. He carried a bamboo cane, wore a long Chinese knife in his belt and in his pockets carried a revolver and a blackjack. Allegedly, Ah Moy Chong had killed three men in California. In Boston, he was not known to have killed anyone but had driven a competitor, Ching Foo of the Ching company, out of Boston at gunpoint after he learned that Ching Foo had offered some South End hoodlums $400 to murder him.

Competition in gambling interests was particularly fierce among the companies. Sometimes one company would issue a formal complaint with the Boston Police over a competitor's gambling operation. Police would raid the gambling room and take dozens of men to the station but, being unfamiliar with the games played, would be unable to distinguish the dealers from the players. Getting information from the Chinese men was futile; they would respond "no savvy" to every question. In the end, the raid did little more than disrupt one night's business for the gambling room, which was the intention of the complainant.

The police were forced to take a closer look at Chinatown in July 1886 when a Chinese man was found brutally murdered in his laundry on Shawmut Avenue in the South End. The affair was so shrouded in mystery that even the victim's name was uncertain. The *Boston Journal* called him Bin Chong; the *Globe*, Ding Chong; the *Post*, Wong Kong. Adding to the confusion, the original owner of the laundry was Quang Sing Kee, and some newspapers used this name. The victim of the "Wash-House Murder," as the papers called the crime, had been a successful gambler and had saved $500, which he planned to take with him to China. He had been a member of the Lee company. The money was missing, but the brutality of the murder—he was stabbed fourteen times—and the fact that his queue had been cut off implied that revenge, either by the Lee company or against it, had been the motive.

The people of Boston were fascinated by the case, and amateur detectives were inundating the police with worthless clues. Three Chinamen were seen looking at daggers in the window of a store on Washington Street; a Chinaman was seen walking fast on Dover Street and frequently turning his head as if he feared he was being followed; five Chinamen were seen boarding a boat to Portland, Maine. The legitimate clues the police were following were not much better. Reliable witnesses saw a man leaving the laundry the night of the murder, but there was no way to find him. Lee Sing, who appeared to match the description, had been unaccounted for the night of the murder and was found packing his trunk to leave the city; he was brought in for questioning. The police brought in three more suspects matching the description but charged none of them.

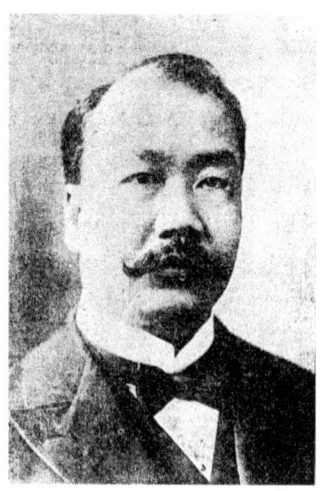

Warry S. Charles. *From* Boston Sunday Post, *August 11, 1907.*

The investigation suffered from the usual complaint: most of the Chinatown residents questioned could not or would not admit to understanding English. Ah Moy Chong was brought in for questioning because he fit the description and his violent reputation was well known to the police, but he had an alibi. Ah Moy Chong spoke fluent English, and before he was released, he expressed the opinion that the killer was not Chinese. He also recommended that the police hire his cousin as an interpreter. They politely declined.

They did, however, bring in a professional interpreter from New York City, a Chinese man who went by the name of Warry S. Charles ("Chinese name" Joe Swen). Charles wore his hair short and dressed in western clothing, and although he was fluent in both languages, he was not fully trusted in Chinatown. He was inclined to think that the murder was premeditated and the killer was Chinese and someone who knew the victim well or he would not have allowed him to remain in the laundry at night. He did not believe the killer was a member of the western hatchet society that had murdered a man in St. Louis a year or so earlier, as some had suggested.

None of the information gathered by Warry Charles brought the police any closer to solving the Wash-House Murder. The case grew colder, and it became apparent to everyone that the murder would never be solved. Before long, the crime faded from memory. The police continued to watch Chinatown and included the rooms on Harrison Avenue in their increasingly frequent gambling raids throughout the city.

Warry Charles decided to remain in Boston, working as an interpreter for the city. He also bought a lucrative laundry on Beacon Hill and became a member of the Sing company, eventually taking a leadership role. Very gradually, Bostonians of Chinese descent spread beyond the bounds of Chinatown to become part of the city at large.

Chapter 10

THE SPORTING LIFE

It seemed as if every man in Boston had gathered on "Newspaper Row" in front of the Washington Street offices of Boston's nine daily newspapers on the morning of February 7, 1882. John L. Sullivan, the "Boston Strong Boy," was fighting Paddy Ryan, bare-knuckled, in Mississippi City, Mississippi, for the heavyweight championship, and the men stood for hours waiting for the papers to post bulletins on their office windows as news of the fight came in by telegraph. Sullivan was the pride of the Boston Irish, a community that had received shabby treatment from the city's elite, and Sullivan's victory over Ryan would be their vindication. But it wasn't just the Irish; Bostonians of every class and nationality were elated by the victory of their favorite son. In fact, Sullivan's victory inspired the nation, and the "Boston Strong Boy" became the first American sports superstar.

Many of the city's moral reformers were endorsing physical sport as a wholesome use of the population's leisure time. The philosophy of "Muscular Christianity" promoted by the Young Men's Christian Association (YMCA) offered sport as a healthy alternative to the dissipating life of the saloon and other dens of sin. The first YMCA in America was founded in Boston in 1851 as a home away from home for sailors and merchants. In the 1880s, the association was headquartered at a large stone building on Boylston Street, complete with a gymnasium. There, physical director Robert J. Roberts developed exercise equipment and a set of exercise routines for which he coined the term "bodybuilding."

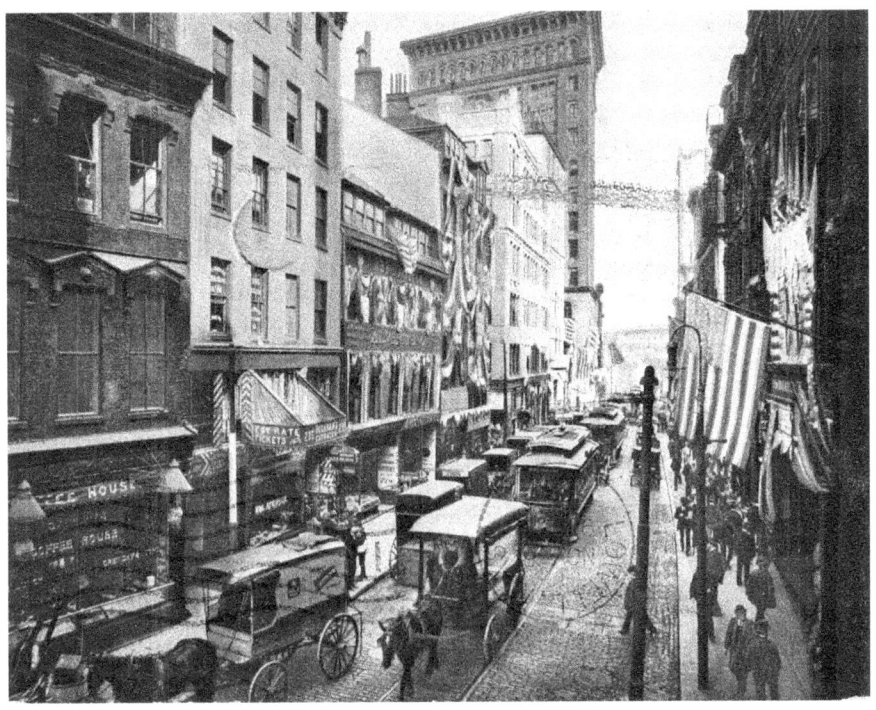

Above: Newspaper Row, postcard. *Author's collection.*

Right: A Boston roller skater. *Author's collection.*

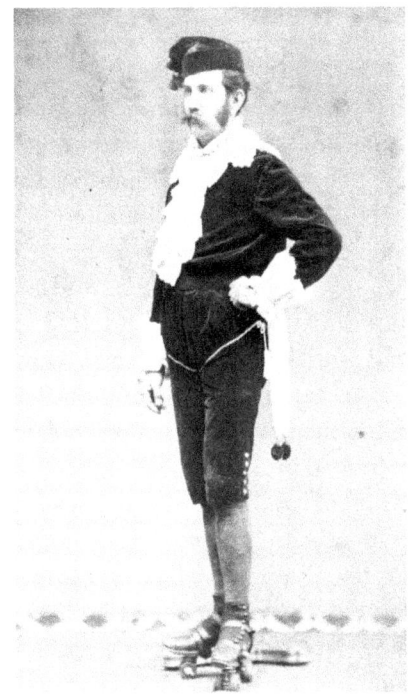

Not all religious leaders viewed sport as healthy, and many popular sports such as baseball and golf were still prohibited by law from being played on Sunday, the only day most working people had available. They warned that public sporting activities led to a mixing of races and classes that resulted in corrupting the pure rather than elevating their opposites. In the 1880s, roller skating had become a popular pastime among young people. After giving cautious approval to public skating rinks in 1884, the Society for the Suppression of Vice reversed its opinion a year later, calling public rinks "the resort of the most disreputable" and claiming that "the saddest instances of seduction and ruin can be traced back to these places."

The life of John L. Sullivan reflected the ambivalent attitude moral reformers held for the sporting life. While a gifted practitioner of his sport and an unquestionably superb example of physical development, he was a champion in a sport that the clergy viewed as sinful and barbaric and that was, in fact, illegal in Massachusetts. Sullivan was also famous as a man of extremely immoderate habits and a living argument against the notion that the gymnasium can replace the saloon.

Though awesome in the ring, outside it Sullivan was not the wholesome, moderate sports hero that the moral community wanted inspiring America's youth. His excessive drinking was legendary. Sullivan said that he had not been much of a drinker before winning the championship, but afterward everyone wanted to buy him a drink. "An ocean would scarcely hold the liquor that was pressed upon me by good fellows," said Sullivan. And from then on, his thirst for liquor became oceanic as well.

On August 7, 1882, hundreds of men gathered once more on Washington Street, this time for the opening of John L. Sullivan's saloon. He had spent $20,000 to convert a storefront into a mahogany palace with a sign in gilt letters that simply read "JOHN L. SULLIVAN." Six bartenders poured beer and whiskey into glasses etched with the champion's monogram. So many feet rested on the brass rail that night that it pulled away from the bar and fell to the floor. The saloon took in $2,900 the first night, and Sullivan had recouped his investment in the first ten days of operation.

John L. Sullivan was a generous man and a soft touch who never turned away a man who could not afford a drink, but he also had a violent and irrational temper, which was only amplified by his drinking. In Boston and around the country, he spent as much time fighting in saloons as he did in boxing rings, and in every case, he greatly outclassed his opponent. Two months after winning the championship fight, he was arrested in Boston for

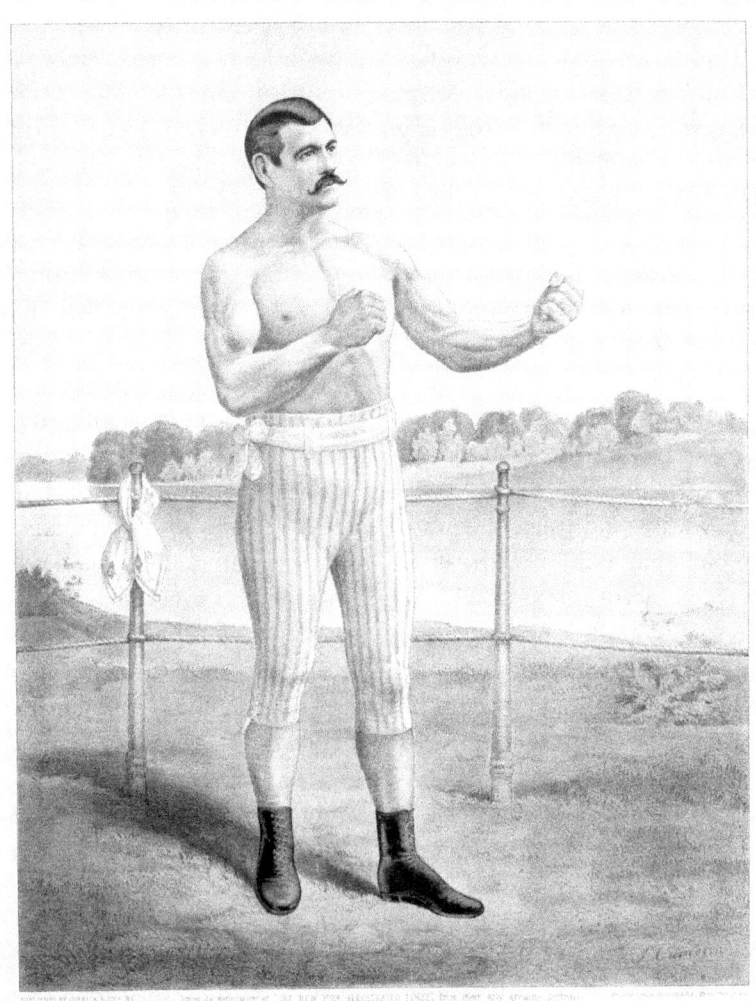

John L. Sullivan. Champion Pugilist of the World, by Nathaniel Currier and James Merritt Ives. *Michele and Donald D'amour Museum of Fine Arts, Springfield, Massachusetts, Gift of Lenore B. and Sidney A. Alpert, supplemented with Museum Acquisition Funds Photography by David Stansbury.*

assault and battery after a barroom fight. He was sentenced to three years in prison but appealed the case and had the verdict overturned.

Just before New Year 1885, Sullivan, driving a two-horse sleigh, parked in front of Yeaton's Saloon on Washington Street. One of the horses jerked and fell down, tipping over the sleigh. Enraged, Sullivan kicked the fallen horse three times below the ribs and then punched the other horse in the face. Inside Yeaton's, Sullivan, still angry, struck a waitress, Rose Booth, with his wet sealskin glove, punched her between the eyes and kicked her as she fled to the kitchen. The matter with the waitress was settled out of court, but the Society for the Prevention of Cruelty to Animals pressed charges, and Sullivan was fined $115.07 for "fast driving and unnecessary cruelty in beating a horse."

The most tragic victim of Sullivan's bullying was his long-suffering wife, Annie, who in May 1885 sued for divorce—not an easy choice for an Irish Catholic woman. The champion often brought his drunken anger home with him and would smash furniture, hurl vile insults at his wife and even hit her. She charged him with "cruel and abusive treatment and gross and confirmed habits of intoxication." Fearing for her life after filing the divorce, she also sought and received a restraining order against her ex-husband.

While Sullivan's bullying did lose him some fans among the more civilized, even the thought of the heavyweight champion beating his wife did not diminish his status among the majority of American sports fans. And in Boston, John L. Sullivan was still seen as a conquering hero. In 1887, the city presented Sullivan a piece of commemorative jewelry of gold and diamonds, created by Tiffany at a cost of $10,000, for his achievement in a sport that was illegal in Boston.

Illegal or not, gymnasiums throughout the city were filled with young men training to be the next John L. Sullivan, but most amateur sportsmen were more likely to practice the popular sport of pedestrianism—long-distance walking. Men could be seen training on the streets at all hours of the day and night. Its most refined form, heel-toe walking, evolved into the modern sport of race walking, but more commonly, pedestrianism involved traveling long distances on foot, either on closed tracks or on the road. In 1861, Edward Payson Weston, paying off an election bet, left the statehouse in Boston on February 22 and walked to Washington, D.C., arriving in time for Abraham Lincoln's inauguration on March 4. Of course, it was not all for fun and exercise; pedestrianism became extremely competitive in the 1870s and 1880s, and where there was competition, there was gambling with all its attending corruption.

In November 1886, a six-day pedestrian race was held at the Columbia Skating Rink on Washington Street. It was a "go-as-you-please" race, meaning contestants could run, jog, trot, walk or use any gait desired, for up to twelve hours a day, around the rink, fourteen laps to the mile. The winner was the man who traveled the farthest in seventy-two hours. The American record at the time was 432 miles. Interspersed with the main race would be periodic sprint races and heel-toe competitions among select contestants. A band was hired to provide music for the full six days.

The race attracted quite a few world-class "peds," as the racers were called. Two local African American men had entered: Frank H. Hart, a former American champion, and James R. Francis, who also competed in six-day roller-skating races. Dan Herty, a famous six-day ped from Revere, Massachusetts, was another local favorite. The field would also include Gus Guerrero from California, who had won a six-day race between men and horses; Dan Burns and Peter Golden of New York City; and Antone Strokle, the current record holder from Michigan. Thomas Patrick Sullivan of Boston would be the "Old Sport" of the race, not really a contender but there to provide some comic relief. Twenty contestants in all went off at 12:15 p.m. on November 1.

The race started with Frank Hart as the favorite—it would be his last race in America before traveling to Australia—but Guerrero and Golden promised tough competition. Hart surprised everyone by dropping out after only ten hours and fifty-five miles. At the end of the first twelve hours, Gus Guerrero was in the lead with a record-breaking eighty-five miles. Guerrero held the lead throughout the race, and as he finished his winning lap, he was presented with a floral star and an elegant gold and black jockey hat, ribbons and sash by Manager E.W. Grant. The "Old Sport" was handed a bouquet of cabbage with a carrot in the middle, and he did a lap around the rink with a bucket over his head while the band played selections from *The Mikado*.

Controversy had surrounded the race from the start. Another six-day race was running at the same time in New Bedford, Massachusetts, and the manager of that race had expected the celebrity peds who ran instead in Boston. He claimed that the Boston race was not really a competition and that the pedestrians were all under salary. While this was not the case, the truth was even more deceptive.

Bose Cobb had conceived the Boston race after viewing a six-day race in New Bedford. Working together with Frank Hart, Cobb put together the deals to make the race happen, and Hart agreed that if he came in first or second, he would split the winnings with Cobb. Cobb made a deal with

Nathan Goodnow, the owner of the Columbia Rink, to rent the space for $250 against 50 percent of the gross receipts. Cobb would pay the prize money from the other 50 percent, less expenses. The visiting peds were told the manager of the race was E.W. Grant, who was actually the janitor of the rink.

Meanwhile, Frank Hart was making deals with the other contestants. Hart, Guerrero, Burns, Golden and Herty agreed to form a combination and evenly divide whatever prize money they received. Hart, realizing that he was over-subscribed, left the race on the first day, and Burns and Herty left the next day. With the combination's membership dwindling, a scheme was devised to boost the score of a ped named Cox and make him a member. As the week progressed, cheating became rampant. Two peds, Elson and Strokle, claimed that Hart had drugged them. On Friday, he brought Elson a bowl of soup, something he had not done before, and Elson was forced to leave the rink with stomach pains and nausea. Strokle claimed that someone had put croton oil, a strong laxative, in his milk, and he lost a day on the track.

Gus Guerrero won the race; Peter Golden came in second; Strokle and Elson took third and fourth. After the finish on Saturday, Grant told the winners and Bose Cobb to be on hand at the rink the next morning at 11:00 a.m. to settle up. Everyone was there Sunday morning except Grant; he sent word that afternoon that he would not be ready to settle until the next morning. When he failed to show on Monday, Cobb went looking for him. He found Grant with Hart and Herty in a room at the Rockingham Hotel, located above the rink, still counting the money and tickets and preparing a statement.

Cobb had paid $133.12 of his own money on railroad fares and board bills for the peds, and he wanted that money paid back. Grant and Hart had not factored that into their calculation and began to hem and haw. Cobb slammed his fist on the table, rattling the coins, and demanded his money.

They had sold 5,671 tickets, total revenue $1,417.80, to be split between the rink and the peds. Expenses for track rental, advertising, money advanced the peds and down payment for the band came out of the rink's share. Grant insisted that $90 still owed to the band, Cobb's $133.12 and other miscellaneous expenses must come from the peds' share. The remaining money, a little over $400, would be divided among the winners: 40 percent for first, 30 percent for second, 20 percent for third, 10 percent for fourth. The winners, however, knew what the gross revenue had been and were expecting to divide $708.90. Grant and

Cobb decided to give Frank Hart the winners' share and send him to explain the situation to them.

Frank Hart knew that he and Herty, who had both left the race early, were no longer considered part of the combination and, under this agreement, would receive nothing. The men left the hotel room together, and at the door of the rink, Grant handed the cashbox to Hart. As Grant and Cobb entered the rink, Hart and Herty made a beeline down Washington Street, cashbox and all. Cobb reported the theft to the police, hoping they could catch Hart before he took a train out of town and a boat to Australia.

The peds took their grievance to Nathan Goodnow, owner of the rink, who informed them that he had provided use of the building but was in no way involved with the race. Grant, who they thought was the manager, was just an employee of the rink. The rink had received its share of the revenue; the money stolen was the winners' share.

The police arrested Hart later that day, and he spent the night in jail, but no one told Bose Cobb. The next day at police court, with no one present to press charges, Hart was released. After a second arrest, the judge ruled the matter a civil case, not a criminal case, and dropped the charges against Hart. Before leaving Boston, Hart told a reporter that he had $414 from the race, and he intended to keep it. He explained the combination the peds had agreed upon and that, on Sunday, the other members had decided to exclude him. "This is my reason for keeping the money," he said, "as I am not going to be played for a fool any longer."

Friends and supporters of Gus Guerrero and Peter Golden organized benefits in their honor, including a variety of athletic exhibitions, burlesque skating acts and foot races among local competitors, raising money so the winners of the six-day race would not leave empty-handed. Bose Cobb recovered the expenses he paid in organizing the event, but the great six-day pedestrian race was a rare example of a failed enterprise on his part.

Chapter 11

SCANDAL

Fred Taber, accompanied by two private detectives, hid outside the Derne Street apartment of his estranged wife, Annie, on August 17, 1885, awaiting the arrival of the Reverend William Downs, pastor of the Bowdoin Square Baptist Church. They watched Downs enter the building, waited a few minutes and then went in after him. Standing outside Mrs. Taber's door, the detectives listened until they heard voices, and then one of the detectives smashed open the locked door with a twenty-pound dumbbell and the other shone a bright lantern into the darkened room. They found both Reverend Downs and Mrs. Taber, shoeless, sitting on the bed—he with his jacket and waistcoat removed, she in just a sack top and short skirt. This was enough for Fred Taber; while the detectives prevented the couple from leaving, he ran for a policeman to have them arrested for adultery.

Implicit in the message of Boston's anti-vice crusaders was the need to protect children and impressionable adults from the corrupting influences of the city's growing lower class. Institutions from the saloon to the public skating rink were decried for the danger they presented in the indiscriminate mixing of social classes. It was the duty of religious and social leaders to set a high example for the young to counter the influence of the criminal class, but their message was increasingly being clouded by sexual and criminal scandals involving the refined and righteous.

If Boston's scandals were an embarrassment to the Society for the Suppression of Vice, they were a source of joy for the *National Police Gazette*, the weekly sporting newspaper published in New York. The *Gazette* was among the publications that the society had successfully removed from the city's train depots, and it had tried to ban the paper completely. This was probably why the *Police Gazette* took such relish in reporting on Boston scandals, referring to the city as a "moral scenter," implying that Boston's morality did not smell so good.

In November 1885, the *Police Gazette* published the story, complete with illustrations, of the sensational divorce proceedings of Mr. and Mrs. Thomas J. Loud. Thomas Loud, a partner at Loud Brothers, a prominent State Street bank, married sixteen-year-old Ellen Mack in May 1881 and took her to the Windsor Hotel in New York City for their honeymoon. Prior to the marriage, Ellen had not been aware that her husband had a violent temper, but she found out soon enough. The morning after the wedding, Loud felt that Ellen was behaving too amorously, so he pulled her off the bed and threw her across the room. When she complained, he told her she ought not mind if he curbed a woman's passion.

The newlyweds had no permanent residence, and when they returned to Boston, they lived in a suite in the Revere House. Mr. Loud was constantly criticizing his wife's behavior and appearance and would physically abuse her to make his point, especially when he was drinking. They held a reception for their friends at the Revere House, and after the guests had left, he chastised Ellen for committing a breach of etiquette—she had shaken hands with a gentleman. Loud struck her in the breast and tried to strangle her. The blow to the breast left her with a persistent pain and had to be attended to by a physician, though she did not tell the doctor what had caused the pain. She finally sent for her father, and she told him, in her husband's presence, about the abuse. Loud, paying no mind to his wife's father, punched Ellen in the face, giving her a bloody nose.

Physical and psychological abuse became a regular feature of their marriage. For a social event, Loud wanted his wife to wear a dress with a low neckline. When she refused, he struck her severely. She finally agreed to wear the dress but once again had to consult a physician as a result of the blow. Once while they were entertaining guests, Loud ordered a bottle of champagne. When Ellen said she did not want to drink, Loud told her if she did not take it one way she should take it in another and then threw the wine in her face. On one occasion, he threatened to pour a bottle of vitriol on her face and had gone so far as to pull the stopper from the bottle when Ellen screamed, and her sister ran into the room and stopped him. On another, he pulled a pistol from under his pillow and threatened to shoot her.

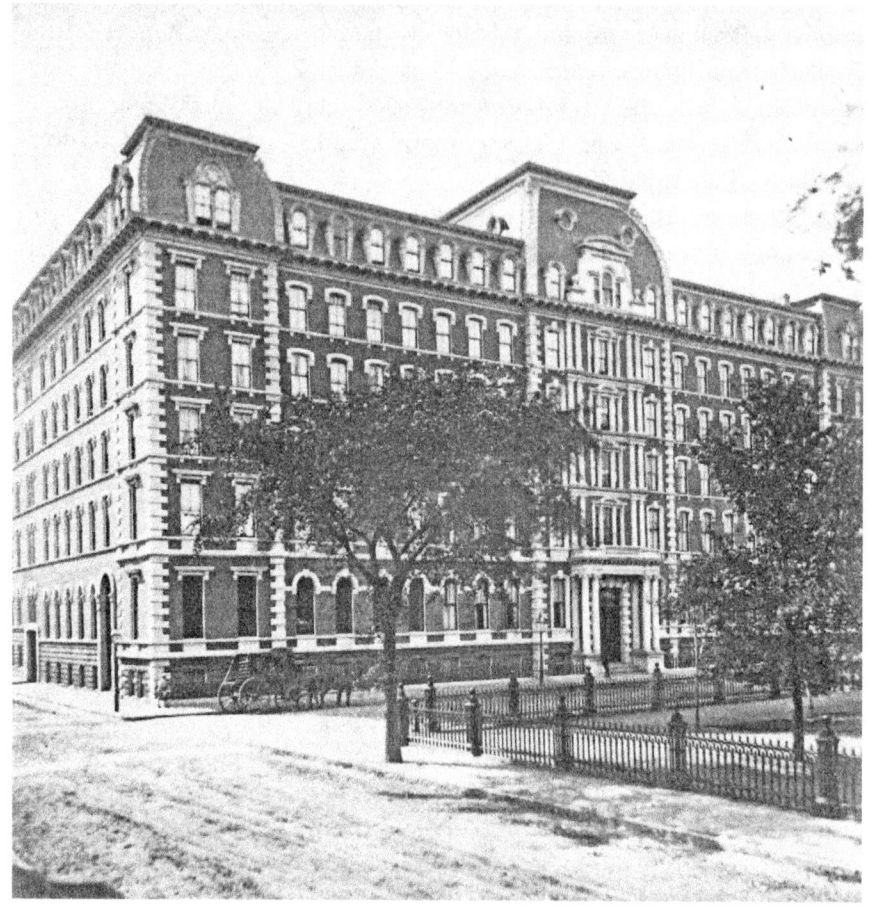

St. James Hotel, postcard. *Author's collection.*

After eleven months at the Revere House, they moved again to the St. James Hotel, and there the abuse intensified. On three occasions, he locked her in the bathroom overnight because she refused to comply with an unreasonable request. Before the marriage, Ellen had been taking violin lessons from Ole Bull, the renowned Norwegian virtuoso, but her husband forbade her from playing and in a fit of rage smashed and burned her violins. He would frequently give her what he called the "Grecian bend kiss," which was performed by grabbing her arms, bending her backward and kicking her with his knee.

They had been married just over a year when Ellen decided that she had had enough. She went to her husband's office and told him she could never go back to him. She fell upon her knees and began to cry. His mother, who had been in the outer office at the time, came in and asked Loud what the matter was. When he told her, his mother said, "Why don't you strike her?" So he did; he hit Ellen across the face. Hysterical and nearly insane, Ellen ran from the office and never went back to her husband.

In 1885, Ellen Loud sued her husband for divorce, and he countersued her for desertion. The trial was short, but it aired all of the Loud family's dirty linen with testimony from Ellen, her sister, her father and various houseguests who had witnessed examples of her husband's cruelty. Thomas Loud had little to offer in his defense, except producing receipts from Jordan Marsh department store to show that he had kept Ellen well furnished during their short marriage. Ellen won the case and obtained a divorce.

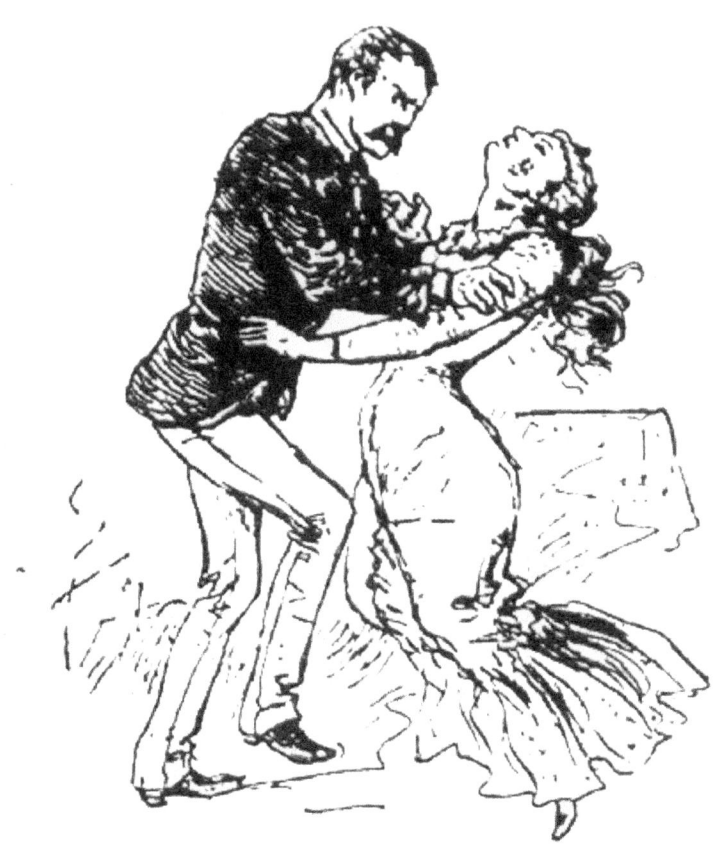

"The Grecian Bend Kiss." *From* National Police Gazette, *November 28, 1885.*

The story of the divorce proceedings and Thomas Loud's cruelties made the front page of newspapers across the country. Editors were especially fascinated by the "Grecian bend kiss" and, under headlines such as "Boston High Life" and "Another Boston Sensation," were pleased to point out that Boston was not as proper as it portrayed itself.

The Loud case generated sensational headlines, but it was nothing compared to the furor raised that same year by Fred Taber catching his wife in a compromising position with the Reverend William Downs. The *National Police Gazette* especially loved exposing hypocrisy among clergymen, so the story of Reverend Downs and Mrs. Taber, a Boston minister caught in bed with one of his parishioners, was irresistible. The *Gazette* published three illustrated features on the Taber-Downs case and several smaller pieces before the matter played out. Daily newspapers around the country followed the story as well.

Reverend Downs became pastor of the Bowdoin Square Baptist Church, one of the oldest Baptist congregations in the city, in October 1880 amid much fanfare and celebration. The energetic young minister, with a wife and eight children, seemed to be exactly what the thriving congregation needed. But as his tenure progressed, not everyone in the church was happy with Parson Downs (as the newspapers called him) and the job he was doing. He had commenced a complete revolution in the church, starting a weekly newspaper called the *Vanguard*, eliminating little luxuries such as a paid choir and committing other, unstated offenses that turned a large faction of the congregation against him. The matter came to a head in January 1885, when some of the prominent members of the church, led by Deacon Wilbur, called for Parson Downs's resignation. When questioned by the press, the churchmen would not specify their reasons but gave vague suggestions of moral transgression by Downs.

Throughout the turmoil, Parson Downs's chief advisor was Fred J. Taber, a well-to-do businessman who owned a food processing company. At the Bowdoin Square Baptist Church, he was a Sunday school teacher and an active member of several church committees. His wife, Annie, also taught Sunday school and served as chairman of the baptismal committee.

After a time, the matter died down, and to the outside world, it appeared as if the members Bowdoin Square Baptist Church had settled their differences. Then the following August, a *Boston Post* reporter received an envelope containing a piece of scrap paper upon which was written one sentence: "More trouble in Bowdoin-square church." The message was not signed, and there was no way to identify the writer, but the information

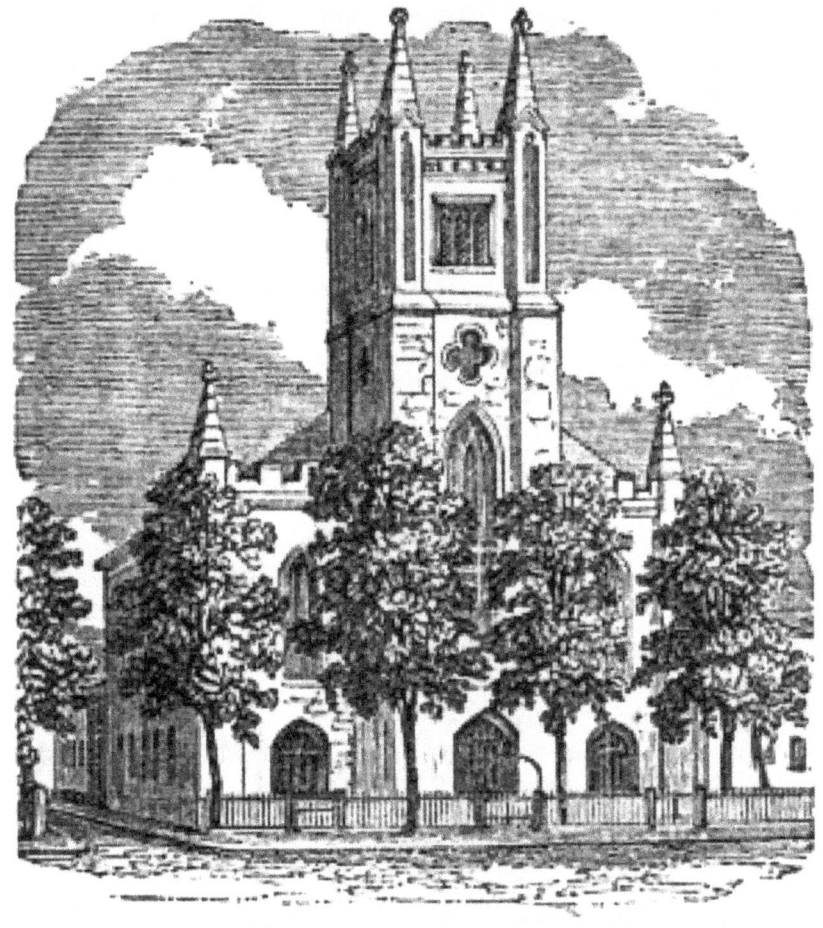

Bowdoin Square Baptist Church. *From* Sketches of Boston, Past and Present, *1851.*

proved correct. Parson Downs's former supporter, Fred Taber, had left the church, and none of his remaining supporters would say why.

Fred Taber had also left his wife, or rather forced her out by selling their house on Tremont Street and telling her she would have to find another place to live. The reason came to light on August 17, when Fred Taber and his hired detectives broke down Mrs. Taber's locked door and found her sitting on the bed with Parson Downs. Neither was fully dressed, and while far from conclusive proof, the situation was suggestive enough to the Victorian mind that both were arrested for adultery and taken to jail.

After the arrests, the dissenting members of the Bowdoin Square Baptist Church admitted that the reason for their opposition was the "undue intimacy" Parson Downs had with female members of the church. When he ignored warnings to desist, the congregation became hopelessly divided. Supporters of Parson Downs said the arrest had been a setup and accused Fred Taber of being jealous to the point of insanity and that opium-eating had made him delusional.

The courtroom was filled to capacity on October 13 when Downs and Taber were scheduled to go to trial. But on that day, the case was continued until November, prompting some to speculate that the case would never be tried but just gradually fade away. This proved to be far from true; the case spawned a multitude of trials that stretched on for years.

While the adultery trial was postponed, the Taber divorce trial, held before Judge Charles Allen, went forward right away. Taber had filed for divorce following the adultery charge, and Mrs. Taber filed a countersuit soon after, alleging that her husband had committed adultery with a woman named Mattie Davidson. It was clear that the marriage was over, but the trial to determine who was at fault would be long and sensational.

Parson Downs testified first and denied that anything untoward had occurred in Mrs. Taber's room that night. He had been helping her pack her bag to travel. The room had been very hot, so he removed his jacket and unbuttoned his vest. He did not think the door was locked and did not remember removing his shoes. Under questioning, Downs admitted that he had called on Mrs. Taber at her apartment more than once and that she had visited his study at the church for spiritual advice. He had also accompanied her on an overnight visit to her mother's house in Worcester.

The sexton at the church testified that Mrs. Taber visited the study five or six times a week and would give a peculiar pull on the door gong to identify herself. Mrs. Jackson, who kept the lodging house on Derne Street where Mrs. Taber resided, said that Downs came by once or twice a week and Mrs. Taber had introduced him as her brother.

The detective who broke down the door said the door had been locked and a towel was hung on the door knob covering the keyhole so no one could peek in. Downs had on only his trousers and shirt, the detective said, and Mrs. Taber had on a wrapper. Both were lying diagonally on the bed.

The most shocking testimony came from Fred Taber, who said he had come home from work early one afternoon and had seen his wife sitting on Parson Downs's lap, and he believed they were kissing. To make sure his suspicions were correct, Taber had gone to the church one time when he

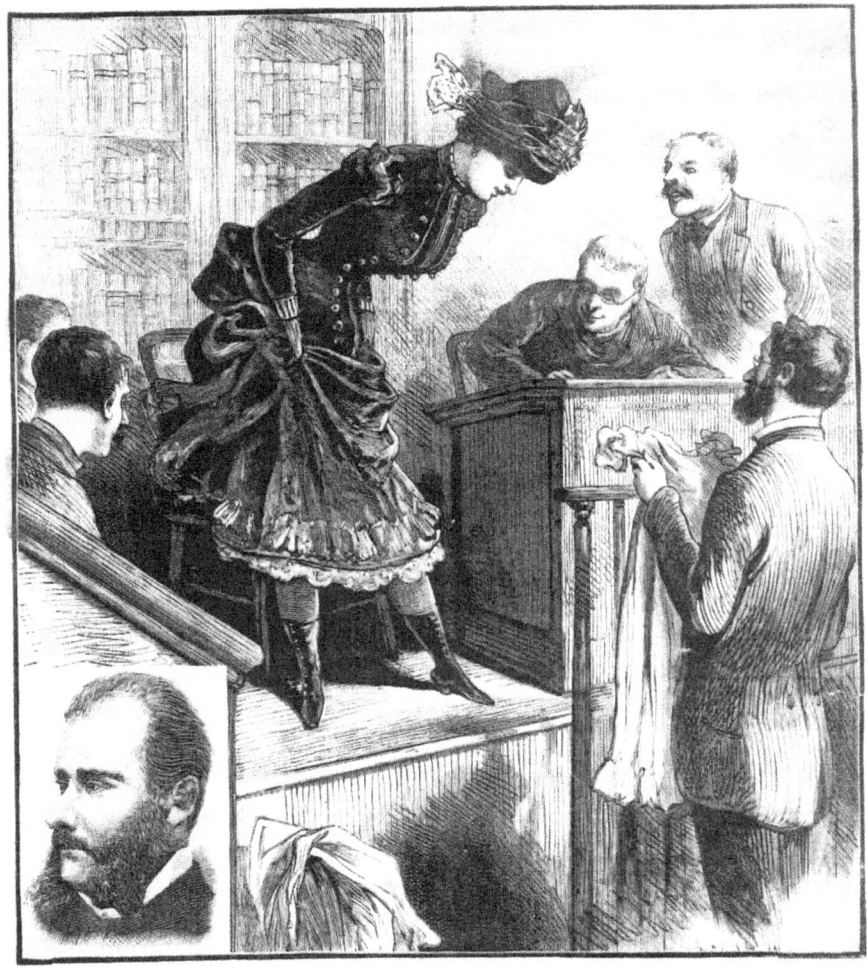

"Is this the dress?" Mrs. Taber Testifies (*inset, Fred Taber*). *From* National Police Gazette, *November 14 1885.*

knew his wife was in Parson Downs's study receiving "spiritual advice." He attached a mirror to the end of his cane and then, standing on a chair, was able to use the mirror to look through the transom and see into the room. He saw his wife and Parson Downs making love. The following day, Taber resigned from the church and told his wife he could no longer live with her.

The trial lasted nearly a month, and forty-five witnesses gave testimony. Interest in the case never died down, and for some sessions, as many as two hundred spectators had to be turned away for lack of space. The ladies of

Boston, in particular, were drawn to the trial. The *Police Gazette* reported, "Women in rich apparel blush behind their handsome fans, and titter audibly at the good points in the evidence."

Many believed that Judge Allen would dismiss both suits, and a group of prominent ministers petitioned the judge not to grant Mr. Taber his divorce because it would result in a "serious blow to religion." But Judge Allen had his own opinions; he granted Mr. Taber's request for a divorce and dismissed Mrs. Taber's.

While the divorce trial was proceeding, the congregation of the Bowdoin Square Baptist Church held a meeting to vote on this resolution drafted by Deacon Wilber: "Resolved, that in view of the disturbances, embarrassments and divisions which have arisen in the relations between this church and Rev. W.W. Downs, the Pastor, he be requested to resign his office at once." The resolution carried 112 votes to 89, but by the rules of the church, Downs could not be forced to resign without proof of gross misdemeanors. There had been many accusations but no proof, and Downs had no intention of resigning.

Parson Downs and Mrs. Taber were anxious for the start of the adultery trial (as were reporters, who could not get enough of the case), but as of February 1886, the prosecution was still looking for some key witnesses, and the case was postponed again.

Downs was kept busy with other matters; he had been locked out of the Bowdoin Square Baptist Church and began holding services at the Music Hall. When his name was omitted from the Massachusetts Baptist Convention's catalogue of ordained ministers in the commonwealth, he sued the secretary, Reverend George W. Bosworth, for $20,000.

Parson Downs became increasingly isolated and distrusting of those around him. On March 1, his attorney, John Coffee, summoned a *Boston Post* reporter named H. Irving Dillenback to his temporary office in the Parker House hotel. Dillenback had interviewed Downs several times and was viewed by Downs and his attorney as someone they could trust until they heard from Mr. Edward Ward of Hartford, Connecticut, that Dillenback had offered to pay him to bring damaging testimony against Downs.

Dillenback denied the charge, but Mr. Ward was in the room when Dillenback arrived at the Parker House. "You have called here for news and been treated like a gentleman," Coffee said to Dillenback. "You have broken bread with us and now you turn on us and ally yourself with the men who are trying to ruin Mr. Downs." At this point, Parson Downs, who was a very athletic man "possessing a pair of biceps which rival Sullivan's in size," grabbed Dillenback by the throat and slapped him across the face. As Dillenback ran for the door, Downs attacked him again, and the two had to be pulled apart.

In May, Mrs. Taber reopened her divorce case, claiming to have new evidence against her husband. She alleged that Fred Taber's former attorney, Mr. Butterworth, had suppressed testimony from Kitty Lincoln and Madeline Miller, who had confessed to adulterous relations with Taber. She claimed that Butterworth himself had committed adultery with Miss Miller and then hidden her away. Judge Allen, who had issued the original verdict, heard this case as well and said, in a nutshell, that he had heard nothing that would change his mind.

That July, Alice Watson, a Sunday school teacher at the Bowdoin Square Baptist Church, accused Parson Downs of being the father of her four-month-old boy and asked the court that he be compelled to pay child support. In August, Joseph Story, one of Downs's chief opponents, was indicted for adultery after a confession from Mrs. Albert Elton of the Bowdoin Square Baptist Church. The same month, Miss Mattie A. Davidson, who had been named as co-respondent in Mrs. Taber's suit against her husband, sued Fred J. Taber for $10,000, alleging seduction.

That December, the district attorney announced that they had been unable to find material witnesses in the adultery case against Parson Downs and Mrs. Taber and declared the indictment nolle prossed, effectively ending the case. This also put an end to the rash of charges and countercharges that had spread through the congregation of the Bowdoin Square Baptist Church.

All that was left now was a suit filed by Parson Downs for unpaid salary against the Bowdoin Street Baptist Church. The amount, $2,562 plus interest, was relatively small, but the issues involved were significant both to Parson Downs and the Baptist Church. Downs was represented by former Massachusetts governor Benjamin Butler, and the case took more than a year to prosecute, reopening all the old wounds in the process. Downs won the first trial but lost the case on appeal.

For each of these events, accusations, lawsuits and trials, newspapers would rehash the cause of the Taber-Downs dispute, invariably under headlines including the words "Boston" and "Scandal." Each new chapter would incrementally diminish the city's ancestral claim to the moral high ground.

Chapter 12

SPIRIT AND FLESH

The great Boston sensation in the spring of 1876 was the execution of the murderer Thomas W. Piper. Four hundred people were crowded inside the Suffolk County Jail to witness the hanging, some paying as much as fifty dollars for a ticket. Outside the jail, another one thousand people stood waiting for the announcement of Piper's death. Thomas Piper had been convicted of a particularly horrendous crime; crazed by laudanum and influenced by "evil literature," he had lured five-year-old Mabel Young up to the belfry of the Warren Avenue Baptist Church and there beat her to death with a cricket bat. After his conviction, Thomas Piper confessed to murdering two other women and attacking a third.

The tragic murder and the triumph of justice provided the sort of dramatic story that had always inspired the poetry of Byron DeWolfe, who had penned ballads on several New England murders. But DeWolfe died in 1873, two years before Mabel Young's murder was committed, so it came as a bit of a shock when a poem written by Byron DeWolfe entitled "Verses Composed on the Confession and Execution of Thomas W. Piper, the Convicted Belfry Murderer" was published in Boston after the execution.

George Gordon Byron DeWolfe was known as the "Wandering Poet of New Hampshire." Though he was born in Nova Scotia and spent much of his time traveling from state to state, DeWolfe called Nashua, New Hampshire, home. He wrote topical poetry about contemporary events, and there was no subject too big or too small for Byron DeWolfe. His poems, printed in Boston as one-page broadsides and sold to the public for a penny a page, commemorated everything from a New Hampshire clambake to the assassination of President Lincoln. DeWolfe was also known as the "Steam-machine Poet" for the rapidity with which he wrote. Sometimes he would include the time it took to write the poem as all or part of the title, for example, "Verses, Given in Twenty Minutes," and "The Great Eastern's Coming. Composed in Forty-three Minutes."

One of the last poems written by Byron DeWolfe was "Verses Composed on the Murder of Miss Kate Leehan" about the brutal murder in Boston of a young Irish immigrant. It is very likely that DeWolfe would have written about Mabel Young's murder as well, had he been alive when it happened, but how had he been able to write "Verses Composed on the Confession and Execution of Thomas W. Piper, the Convicted Belfry Murderer" after his death? In a column down the middle of the printed broadside, between two columns of verse, was the answer:

A FEW WORDS TO THE READER

The public will doubtless remember the wandering Poet Byron DeWolfe of Nashua, N.H., who passed away some five years ago of congestion of the lungs; he still seems to feel his presence needed here in regard to composing Poetry on various subjects, as he was in the habit of Doing while here on this earth and has selected the medium Miss Lillie as the most reliable and powerful medium to control. I wish it to be distinctly understood that these verses were composed by me Byron DeWolfe, through the mediumship of Miss Lillie, the Physical and test medium in about 2 hours and a half. Parties wishing to consult the medium will find her one of the best test mediums the world can produce; she is an independent medium. Her present place of business is 35 Hanover St., where she can be seen and consulted. Byron DeWolfe.

Reading "Verses Composed on the Confession and Execution of Thomas W. Piper, the Convicted Belfry Murderer," it does not take a literary critic to tell that, in death, the Wandering Poet had lost his chops. The Kate Leehan poem explores the character and thoughts of the victim, but the Thomas Piper poem is little more than a rhyming recitation of facts. One verse is lifted verbatim, but for the name, from the Kate Leehan poem:

Strew flowers over Mabel's [Kate's] form,
Which now the earth does cover.

Her spirit's free from every harm!
God is her kindest lover!

And nothing in the Kate Leehan poem approaches the awkwardness of this verse from "Thomas W. Piper":

Sleep, mangled form, in the cold earth be sleeping;
Rest, gentle spirit, in sunshine and love;
Mother afflicted, O, answer though weeping,
Don't Mabel now wait for your coming, above?

DeWolfe's medium was Miss Lillie Darling, who advertised in the *Boston Herald* classifieds under the heading "Clairvoyants &c." She was a "test medium," meaning that she was able to communicate with spirits on subjects known only to the deceased and the questioner. She was also a stage performer. In May 1875, she advertised a performance in Salem, Massachusetts, promising "Startling Manifestations," including the raising of a piano by spirit power, instruments played while she is bound, spirit flowers brought and materialization of spiritual forms, faces and hands.

A reviewer for the *Salem Register* was not impressed by Miss Lillie's show. The exhibition, he said, "did not give perfect satisfaction to anybody." The crowd was too small to please the management, and the performance did not live up to the advertisements. Apparently, the piano raising was not visible to the audience. "There were some cabinet manifestations that were pretty clever, but as a whole, the exhibition was a failure."

In July 1875, Miss Lillie appeared in a public séance held at the Boston Theater featuring several mediums, who, it was alleged, were preparing to appear before a scientific commission at St. Petersburg, Russia. The audience was made up of at least as many skeptics as believers, and when Miss Lillie appeared on stage, she could not be heard over the boos and catcalls.

The performance prompted a response from Madam H.P. Blavatsky and Colonel Henry S. Olcott, spiritualists and representatives of the Academy of Sciences attached to the Imperial University of St. Petersburg. In a scathing letter to the Boston press, Madam Blavatsky and Colonel Olcott included a list of mediums who definitely had not been selected to display their powers in Russia. The list included Miss Lillie Darling. "The Imperial University of St. Petersburg makes its investigation in the interest of science," they wrote, "not to assist charlatans to give juggling performances in theaters, upon the strength of our certificates."

Apparently, the Wandering Poet of New Hampshire was also dissatisfied with Miss Lillie's medium work. Byron DeWolfe never again used her services, and he never again published a poem from beyond the grave.

Spiritualism was popular in Boston, as it was throughout the country, during the Victorian era. Spiritualistic practitioners fell into two categories: those like Madam Blavatsky and Colonel Olcott, who viewed spiritualism as a serious metaphysical philosophy and worked to reconcile their beliefs with science and traditional religion, and those like Miss Lillie Darling, who used it as a tool to make a fast buck off a gullible populace.

Boston was a major center of activity for serious believers in spiritualism. The oldest and longest-running spiritualist newspaper, the *Banner of Light*, began publication in Boston in the 1850s. In 1885, the First Spiritual Temple, a magnificent stone Romanesque building that still stands on the corner of Newbury and Exeter Streets, was built with money contributed by wealthy wholesale grocer Marcellus S. Ayer. The temple included a 1,500-seat auditorium, seven lecture suites, a library, a reading room and a kitchen.

The city was also home to a huge array of spiritual mediums of dubious authenticity. An average edition of the *Boston Herald* would include classified advertisements for Miss Lillie Darling, Mrs. Franks, Professor Judson, Madam Bishop, Anael and thirty or more other clairvoyants, offering advice on health, marriage, business and love, promising to find lost friends and property and to "tell your life from cradle to grave."

Sometimes the line between serious spiritualists and charlatans was not sharply drawn. In the 1850s, a Harvard divinity student named Frederick L.H. Willis, on an ocean voyage for his health, began to hear rapping sounds in his stateroom, and in each instance, he was compelled to reminisce about two of his friends who had died. When back in Boston, he consulted with spiritualists who convinced Willis that he was a spiritual medium. Willis honed his powers and began giving public séances. He would channel the spirits of Byron, Shelley and other dead poets and would cause musical instruments to play recognizable tunes underneath the table, untouched by living humans.

In 1857, a Harvard engineering professor named Henry Eustis attended two of Willis's séances. In the second one, a drum beneath the table played a rhythm recognizable as that of "Hail Columbia." Suddenly, Professor Eustis reached under the table and grabbed Willis's foot, saying he had been using his foot to produce the sounds. Willis denied the charge, but the damage was done. The Harvard divinity school, unhappy in the first place to have a spiritualist in their midst, would not tolerate a fraudulent one and expelled Frederick Willis.

The *Banner of Light* came to Willis's defense, but for the most part, the mainstream press supported Harvard's decision. The controversy fueled renewed interest in spiritualism in Boston, and the *Boston Courier* offered a $500 reward for any medium who could produce spirit rapping or table tipping in a controlled environment under the watchful eye of a committee of Harvard professors. Dr. Henry Gardner, a noted Boston spiritualist, took the challenge. Gardner brought some of America's most renowned spiritual mediums, including the founders of modern spiritualism, the Fox sisters (who would later admit that they defrauded their followers for years). None was able to satisfy the committee, and the prize went unclaimed.

Though Frederick Willis went on to have a successful career as a physician, he always maintained that his powers were real and the manifestations were genuine. To this day, many spiritualists believe that Willis was a true medium who was treated unfairly.

To mainstream Protestant ministers, spiritualism in any form was an abomination serving only the devil. They preached from the pulpit that all true Christians must fight against this heresy. But many in their congregations disagreed and followed a tradition that had actually begun with Boston's Puritan settlers. They were sincere Christians who occasionally dabbled in the occult, using sieves, scissors and candles to foretell the future. Cotton Mather, a Puritan minister famous for his role in the Salem witch trials, referred to them as "little sorceries."

To Reverend Henry Morgan, all mediums and clairvoyants were frauds at best. In *Boston Inside Out!*, Frank Gildersleeve takes a reluctant Minnie Marsden to have her fortune told by a clairvoyant medium. He describes the medium as a woman trying to look young, but "notwithstanding the paint and powder, the ruffles and fizzes, the 'idiot fringe' and the paste and plated jewelry, the lines on the brow, the crows' feet under the eyes, the scraggy neck and attenuated bust, all told a tale of Time." Reading tea leaves and cards, and through a trance where she channels the spirit of Hahahoopahoopa, the great medicine man of the six nations, the medium tells Minnie what Frank has already paid her to recite: that she sees Frank and Minnie happily together, with a love so strong that a formal marriage is irrelevant and meaningless.

Morgan put quack doctors in the same category as clairvoyants and claimed that there were two hundred quacks practicing in Boston, and only about a dozen had graduated from any institution except penal ones.

They had been arrested for murder, passing obscene literature, forgery, counterfeiting and so on. Some crossed into the realm of spiritualism, curing by the "laying on of hands." In one case, an electric battery was used to facilitate communication with the spirit world. For five dollars a touch, the healing sparks of life oozed from his fingers.

Boston's most flamboyant quack was Dr. Charles L. Blood, the inventor of oxygenized air. While most quacks kept a low profile, relying on word-of-mouth referrals, and were prepared to close up shop at a moment's notice, Dr. Blood advertised heavily in local newspapers, sometimes taking up one or two full columns with his name and office address featured prominently.

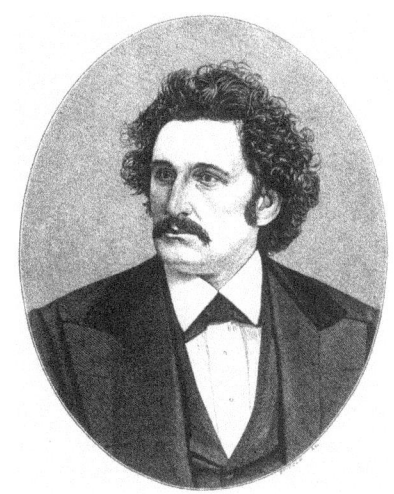

Dr. Charles L. Blood. *Wikimedia Commons.*

Blood came to Boston around 1865 and set up an office on Harrison Avenue where he began treating patients with his great discovery, oxygenized air, a cure for impure conditions of the blood; all diseases of the nose, throat and lungs; paralysis; epilepsy; neuralgia; rheumatism; and scrofula. Dr. Blood was a tall, imposing man, with dark eyes and an engaging manner, calculated to instill confidence. Patients were ushered into a sumptuously decorated treatment room, and Dr. Blood himself applied the oxygenized air.

In 1866, Dr. Blood's practice was booming; patients raved about how good they felt after being treated with oxygenized air. It's not surprising; oxygenized air was nothing more than nitrous oxide—laughing gas—commonly used by dentists as an anesthetic. The problem was, nitrous oxide has no lasting effect and is not a cure for anything. At the peak of his success, Dr. Blood franchised his treatment, supplying other doctors with oxygenized air, but refused to reveal the "formula."

Before long, a physician named Dr. Jerome Harris figured out what Dr. Blood was up to. But rather than exposing the fraud, Harris set up an office not far from Blood's, brought in his own tanks of nitrous oxide and called his treatment superoxygenized air. Dr. Blood did not like the competition and dealt with it right away. He sent a henchman to Dr. Harris, calling himself Mr. Carvill from Lewiston, Maine. Carvill suffered from bronchial trouble and came to Dr. Harris specifically to take advantage of superoxygenized air, but as soon as the treatment was administered, Mr. Carvill fell to the floor in a fit. He rolled around, frothing at the mouth and writhing in contortions as if in great pain. As soon as he was able to be moved, Dr. Harris took him home in a carriage.

The next day, the newspapers contained vivid accounts of the "poisoning" of a man named Carvill by superoxygenized air. It was reported that the patient was still in danger, and Dr. Blood made sure the reporters were frequently updated as to his condition. At the same time, he assured the public that the perfectly harmless oxygenized air continued to be administered at his Harrison Avenue office.

Dr. Blood was a master at reading a situation, knowing when to leave and how to disappear unobtrusively. He profited from oxygenized air for more than a decade, and then, sensing that the time was right, he sold his practice to Frank M. Natic for $3,000 and left Boston.

In different cities, under different names, Dr. Blood employed similar schemes, setting up medical practices and then selling them. In Washington, D.C., he distributed pamphlets saying that $30,000 in prize money would be distributed, in amounts ranging from $200 to $500, to people chosen at random from those who bought the medical book he was selling. Of course, there was no prize money.

He was arrested for the prize scheme in Philadelphia in 1883. Because of an open warrant in Boston, Blood was turned over to Massachusetts state detectives and extradited to Boston. He would answer charges placed by Frank Natic, who said the medicines sold to him by Blood proved to be of no value. Blood was released on $5,000 bail, and then he left the state and went straight back to Philadelphia. From there, he went to New York, where he was arrested again, this time for selling patent medicines without a proper revenue stamp. He was held on $50,000 bail.

As soon as he could, Dr. Blood dropped out of sight again, but his name would pop up from time to time, in and out of Boston—as a witness in a divorce, a suspect in a blackmail case, a person of interest in a New Hampshire murder. But he never served any prison time.

From Reverend Morgan's point of view, the main complaint against both mediums and quacks was not their fraudulent practices; it was their unadvertised services. In most American cities, it was a well-known secret (at least among those who needed to know) that spiritualistic mediums could provide drugs and herbs to end pregnancies, as well as abortion operations or entrée to baby farms—secret hospitals where an unwed mother could give birth in private and leave her trouble behind. Unlicensed doctors were most likely to perform the abortions—"pre-natal murders," in Morgan's words—or deliver the unwanted babies.

Like prostitution, abortion and running baby farms were offenses that both police and prosecutors tried to avoid and only the most extreme reformers, like Reverend Morgan, would speak of in public. His fictional description of the trial of a woman accused of baby farming includes a none-too-subtle indictment of the judge and prosecutor in the testimony of the accused:

> *"What would city folks do without me? What would you do, Mr. Judge?"*
> *And the judge colored and blushed and tried to smile.*
> *"And what would you do, gentlemen attorneys?"*
> *And the attorneys blushed and tried to smile. Then said the judge to the attorneys, "Do you wish to persecute this poor woman?"*
> *"Oh, no! No! No! Your Honor! We wish nothing of the sort."*
> *"Then I will place the case on file, and let her go on her own recognizance without bail."*

Unless the woman died, abortion cases were seldom reported in Boston. The only major baby farm case actually involved a legitimate charity institution in Holliston, a suburb southwest of Boston, where many unwanted Boston babies ended up. When one infant died, the press hurled charges of baby farming, and the matron was charged with murder. The real baby farms operated in secret and were hotbeds of infanticide and blackmail and, as Reverend Morgan implied, were left unprosecuted.

For the most part, though, spiritualistic mediums and quack doctors served the same role in Victorian Boston as they do today: they brought short-term hope and comfort to those in need and income to the unscrupulous.

Chapter 13

THE WICKEDEST MAN IN BOSTON

*O*ne June night in 1884, Carl A. Trundy, an agent for the Society for the Suppression of Vice, stood outside the Dime Museum on Tremont Row, waiting for two of his associates. They were on assignment from Agent Henry Chase, the operational head of the society, to visit a number of saloons suspected of engaging in gambling and report any evidence that could be used against them. The agents were given a small sum of money so they could sit in on a hand or two and gather enough information to file a complaint with the police. Trundy was to join them for the last stop of the night, Bose Cobb's saloon and dance hall on Norman Street, which they planned to visit at around 11:00 p.m.

Trundy waited past the appointed hour, and when the men had not made an appearance, he became alarmed, thinking that they may have had some difficulty at one of the resorts they had planned to visit. He went to hunt them up, visiting several saloons in the South End and West End on his way to Norman Street. He had no luck finding his associates and ended up going into Bose Cobb's alone.

Amid the din and confusion of the dance hall, Trundy was approached by one of the "female inmates," the usual welcome at Cobb's, and Trundy, not wanting to appear out of place, agreed to have a drink with her—just a tonic, though, he would later specify. Then Trundy went upstairs, where he believed he would find a faro layout, roulette wheel and dice games in progress. Quite a few people in the upstairs apartment were drinking and conversing, but no one was gambling. Gradually, each left the room and went downstairs until the only people left were Trundy and an angry-looking African American man. Trundy went downstairs, and the man followed closely behind him. Realizing that his mission had failed, Trundy went back outside.

As he walked down Norman Street, Trundy heard two men rapidly approaching him. One of them called out to him, "Hullo, Boss!" Trundy turned around to see two more black men. One of them flashed a lantern in his face, and the other man hit Trundy behind the right ear with a slungshot—a nautical tool consisting of a heavy weight tied to a cord. "Now git!" said the man as Trundy fell to the ground.

Trundy had no recollection of how he managed to get to the train station to return to his home in Watertown, but the following day, he lay in his bed with a lump on the side of his head the size of an egg and was so sick that he believed he was dying. Police Inspector Hanscom and Dr. Jenks, chairman of the police commissioners, traveled to Watertown to hear Trundy's antemortem statement. They arrived to find that Trudy's condition had been greatly exaggerated and his recovery was assured.

Bose Cobb denied any connection to the incident and believed that Trundy had made up the story. The police agreed; when they investigated Trundy's story, they concluded that he must have been considerably under the influence of alcohol the night of the incident. They traced his movements that night and found that he had stopped at Nelligan's Saloon on Harrison Avenue, where he ordered four or five drinks. Someone who had seen him on his return to Watertown said that his breath smelled strongly of rum. Trundy claimed that he had, for appearance's sake, two drinks at Nelligan's and secretly poured the others into the cuspidor. When he was at Cobb's, his female companion had urged him to try some of the cherry rum she was drinking. He took only a sip, but that explained the rum on his breath.

To the Society for the Suppression of Vice, this was just another example of the police protecting a known gambling house. Someone had informed Bose Cobb that their agent would be there gathering evidence and had not only suspended gambling operations for the night but had assaulted the agent. Instead of investigating Cobb, the police turned their focus on Trundy, publicly tarnishing the reputation of an honest, sober man. The society related the incident in its annual report and called Bose Cobb's "one of the worst places in the city."

By 1885, Bose Cobb had been a notorious public figure in Boston for well over ten years. The *Boston Globe* had called him "the wickedest man in Boston," and his name was frequently in all the Boston papers in stories

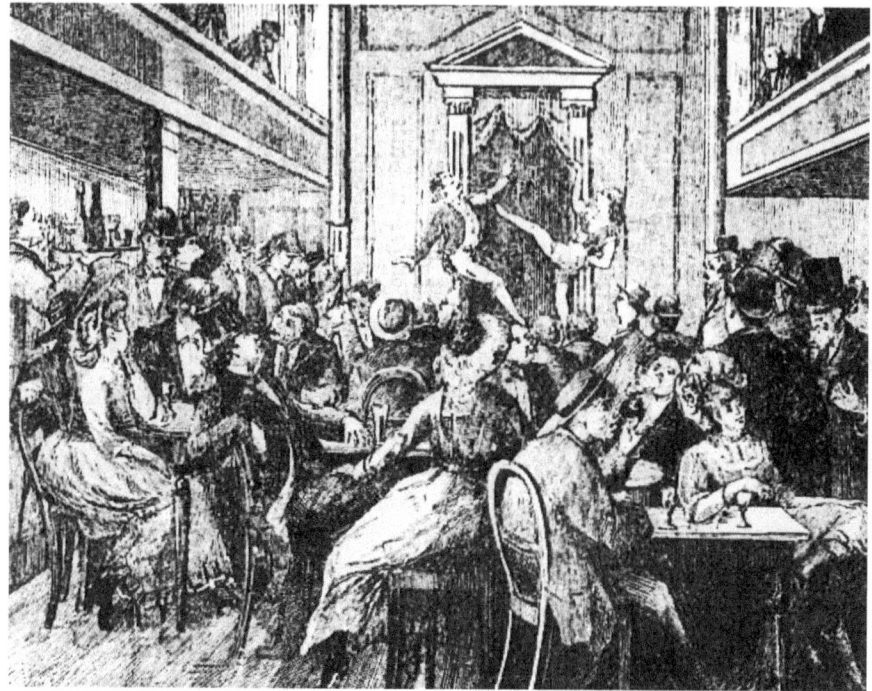

A free-and-easy. *From* Theatrical and Circus Life, *1882.*

relating to vice or violence. Cobb was involved in gambling of every sort, owned several brothels, paid no attention to liquor laws and associated with known criminals. And the Society for the Suppression of Vice was correct; he did it all with the full knowledge of the Boston Police.

Emery Boardman Cobb, better known as "Bose," was an African American man born in 1837 in Natick, Massachusetts, west of Boston. He was born free; the Massachusetts Constitution effectively abolished slavery in 1787, so it is likely that his parents were born free as well. His accent would have been pure Massachusetts, with none of the drawl and twang of the freed slaves who made up most of Boston's black population after the Civil War.

Like his father and brother, Bose Cobb worked in the shoe factories of Natick, but he was too restless for mill work. After a brief term in the house of correction, he enlisted in Company K of the U.S. Colored Troops, Twenty-Third Infantry Regiment, and fought for the Union in the Civil War. In 1864, he mustered out in Boston and settled in the vice district known as the Black Sea, where he ran a regular dice game. He was soon part owner of the

Bella Union Dance Hall on North Street, frequented by men and women, both black and white, "of the very lowest character." A number of murders were committed there, but Cobb was never implicated.

Cobb also became involved in prostitution and ran a brothel at 5 Eaton Place in the West End. In 1876, a coordinated police raid on five houses of ill fame included the Eaton Place resort. By this time, the name Bose Cobb was well known in Boston, and the papers reported that he was said to be the owner. He was always careful to make sure that he was never present when raids or arrests were being made.

As the police began to crack down on the Black Sea, Bose Cobb moved the center of his operations to a dance hall on the corner of Norman and Gouch Streets in the West End. If the dance hall had a formal name, it was never published; the newspapers always referred to it as Bose Cobb's dance hall or just Cobb's place. At its peak, the resort was known by sporting men throughout America as "the village" because it consisted of six buildings on Norman Street. The main building housed a saloon and dance hall on the first floor; faro, dice and other gambling games on the second floor; and high-stakes table games on the third floor. The complex also included five houses of prostitution, all connected by tunnels.

Gambling and prostitution were unquestionably illegal in Boston, but the saloon and dance hall also functioned in violation of most of the city's liquor laws. The place stayed open on Sunday, did not honor any mandated closing time and charged admission at the door, which was expressly illegal. It was illegal to serve alcohol in any room where there was music and dancing because the city wanted to prevent the types of rowdy music halls that were popular in Chicago and farther west. Cobb's had a folding wall that could be employed to separate dancing and drinking if they expected a raid, but most of the time the room was wide open. The proprietor made sure that girls were always available for any man who wanted to dance, and the rule was that after each number, the couple would dance to the bar, and the man would buy them each a drink. This practice was also explicitly illegal.

They did the cakewalk, a popular African American dance, to the music of a piano, fiddle and other instruments when available, led by the master of ceremonies, James "Jumping Jim" Henderson. "Jumping Jim" was more than just the exuberant leader of the cakewalk; he was the hands-on manager of the dance hall, as well as the head of security. Cobb did not always have advance knowledge of police raids, and Henderson had to be ready to hide illegal activity at a moment's notice. Sentries were posted around the dance hall who could communicate danger by a switch outside connected to an electric bell at the bar. The bar was connected to the gambling rooms by electric bells and speaking tubes. An iron door to the gambling rooms could be closed to keep the police out, at least as long as it took to hide the gaming equipment.

But Cobb seldom needed these extreme measures. It was said that he spent a small fortune on police officers to stay informed of planned raids. He also stayed on the good side of the police by helping them out with information on thieves and fugitives who passed through his dance hall. While Cobb was always loyal to his own people, he had no compunction about giving up someone outside his circle. This arrangement worked well for Cobb and the police, but the Society for the Suppression of Vice was not happy. It complained that prior to the incident with Trundy, the police had performed three separate raids on Cobb's place but found no illegal activity and made no arrests.

Bose Cobb was a tall, good-looking man, well dressed with a gentlemanly bearing. He in no way resembled his clientele and was, as the *Boston Herald* said, "about the last man anyone would pick out for a 'dive' keeper." While still living in Natick, he married a woman named Sarah Howard, and they had a daughter, Nellie. They were still together in Boston in 1870, but after that, it is unclear what became of Sarah. Reportedly, he married at least two more times, each time to a white woman. Other accounts say he kept a harem of beautiful white women. In any case, Bose Cobb had several more children, but Nellie remained his favorite.

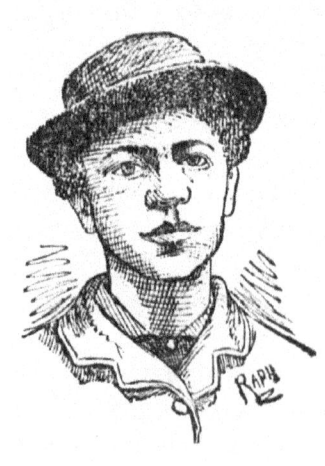

James Francis. *From* Boston Sunday Globe, *May 17, 1885.*

In his heyday, Cobb spent money freely and lived an extravagant lifestyle. He had a stable of fast horses, and in the wintertime, he hitched one up to his double-runner sleigh, which he called Mount Auburn. He would speed down Beacon and Park Streets and didn't mind when young boys sat on the runners and rode along. He called the sleigh Mount Auburn because, at the speed he traveled, if the sleigh ever tipped over, everyone on it would end up in Mount Auburn Cemetery. In 1885, Bose Cobb bankrolled a young African American roller skater for a six-day skating race at Madison Square Garden in New York. Cobb was in attendance as his protégé, seventeen-year-old James Francis, took a respectable fifth place.

In 1885, a joint commission of the Massachusetts state legislature held hearings on the question of transferring authority over the board of police commissioners from the mayor to the governor. The hearings gave the Society for the Suppression of Vice and other reform groups an opportunity to air their grievances against the Boston Police Department. Agent Chase related numerous instances where saloons were given advance information of police raids and presented results of their investigation into violations of Sunday closing laws. Their protests were not unopposed; Senator Wright asked if the society had taken out a warrant on the Somerset Club House, referring to a private gentlemen's club in Boston where liquor was regularly served on Sunday. But in the end, the status quo was changed, and the legislature agreed that appointment of police commissioners and enforcement of liquor laws would be placed under the state governor.

The changes resulted in major reorganization within the police department. Captain Timothy Hurley, Lieutenant Henry Dawson and Sergeant Lawrence Cain replaced existing men at Station 3 with the goal of cleaning up the West End, specifically closing down Bose Cobb. Sergeant Cain, who retired as a captain fourteen years later, recalled the events surrounding his transfer:

> *I am not saying that this is so, but it seemed to be understood that I was transferred to station 3 for a purpose.*
>
> *That was about 14 years ago. I had not been at station 3 only a short time when I met "Bose Cobb" on the street. We greeted each other pleasantly enough, and I was about to pass on when he stopped me.*
>
> *"See here sergeant," said he, "I understand you've been sent down here to clean me out."*
>
> *I acknowledged that that might be the case.*
>
> *"Well, sergeant," said he, "don't you know they have been trying to do that for 29 years and haven't succeeded yet?" Then he laughed as if it was a pretty good joke. I allowed that what he said was probably true, but I assured him that I was going to clean him out and that while he might laugh then, I would have the laugh later.*

In spite of his cocky attitude with Sergeant Cain, Bose Cobb was worried. The protection that he had bought through years of payoffs and gestures of goodwill had all been transferred away, and the new regime would be, at least in the short run, focused and incorruptible. The next raid on the dance hall would be the real thing. Cobb officially and very publicly transferred ownership of the dance hall to his right-hand man, "Jumping Jim" Henderson, and started planning his move out of the West End.

The night of September 5, 1885, Bose Cobb left the dance hall just before 10:30 p.m. The new owner was leading a cakewalk and happily presiding over a healthy Saturday night crowd. As Cobb walked down Gouch Street, the music from the dance hall filling the air, he barely noticed a large furniture wagon lumbering down the road in the other direction. The wagon stopped outside the dance hall entrance and immediately at least a dozen uniformed police officers poured from the back of the wagon and rushed into the dance hall. The sentries were taken completely by surprise; they had no time to ring the alarm bells. Inside, police officers in civilian clothes who had been waiting on the dance floor and at the gaming tables sprang into action to prevent employees from hiding any signs of infraction or closing the iron doors.

The place erupted in confusion as customers tried to leave or hide to avoid arrest. Those who had been gambling upstairs climbed the stairs even farther until they were standing on the flat roof of the building. There, the most agile leaped to the roofs of adjoining buildings, and the rest stood waiting to see what would happen next. But the police were not interested in customers that night; they had warrants for violation of liquor laws, and they were there to arrest the proprietor and his employees.

Gambling was the most serious offense for an establishment selling liquor, and while they did not find a game in progress, the police took sledgehammers to faro tables and other gambling paraphernalia in plain sight on the second floor. On the third floor, they found and confiscated a cache of illegal liquor.

"Jumping Jim," along with the two bartenders on duty, Kate Mansfield and James Winslow, surrendered gracefully to the inevitable. At least fifteen women, both black and white, ranging in age from fifteen to thirty-nine, were arrested and marched into black Mariahs that arrived shortly after the raid began.

The raid had been organized in extreme secrecy. Sergeant Cain earlier in the day had arranged to use the wagon of a local furniture dealer. The arresting officers were told to muster that evening on Mount Vernon Street near the statehouse but were not told their mission. Some believed that they would be breaking up a dogfight in the North End. The wagon took a circuitous route to Norman Street so as not to raise any suspicions. When they arrived at Bose Cobb's, the men were given their orders.

Regardless of who officially owned the dance hall, the police stated that they had hoped to catch Bose Cobb himself in the raid. Once again, the Wickedest Man had walked away early and avoided arrest.

Chapter 14

JOHN BULL AND
THE MELLEN CONSPIRACY

The raid on Bose Cobb's dance hall was intended to break up the retreat and prevent it from transferring to another part of the city, but the following Monday night, "Jumping Jim" had the place up and running at the usual location with a larger-than-usual crowd. Though not technically the owner anymore, Bose Cobb still used the dance hall as his headquarters, but it soon became apparent the place had become too notorious for his safety.

In October 1885, a woman calling herself Mrs. Hamilton paid a visit to the dance hall and requested a private meeting with Bose Cobb. She explained that a friend of hers would pay a large sum of money to have someone in Baltimore murdered and thought Cobb could help her find a man for the job. While Bose Cobb's connections probably included some who could accommodate this request, murder for hire was not really his line. Besides, he had the distinct feeling that the police were setting him up for an arrest. Wanting to learn more, he told Mrs. Hamilton that he would help her and then set up a meeting with a private detective named John Bull.

"John Bull" was the alias of James Donahoe, a fringe character in Boston with a shady reputation of his own. At the time, he was working as a dealer in the dance hall. Donahoe was born in London and came to America with his parents when he was eight years old. He had worked as a Boston Police detective, a gambler and a dealer in stolen merchandise before becoming a private detective. Tall and strong, fearless and vindictive, he earned the nickname John Bull because of his birthplace after thrashing

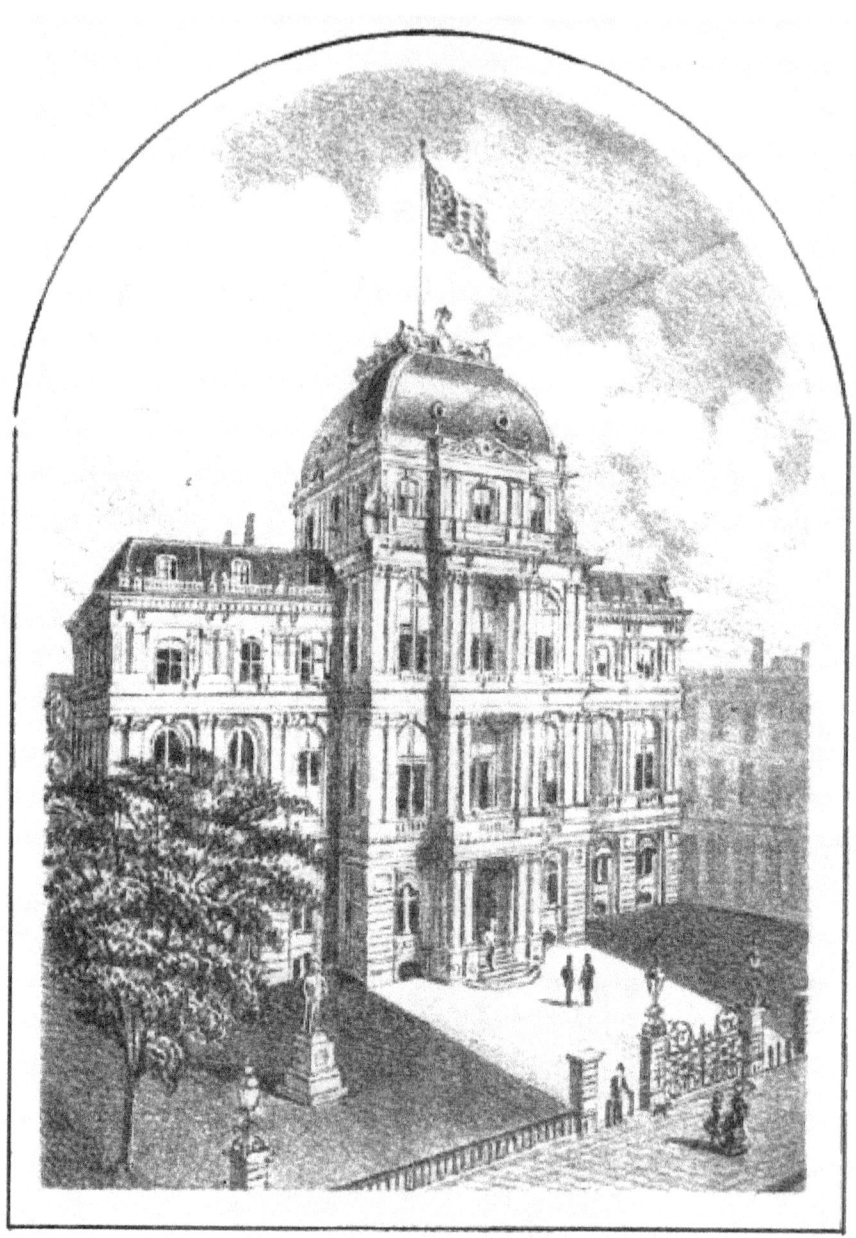

Boston City Hall. *From* Police Records and Recollections, *1873.*

a noted prizefighter. In his detective work, John Bull would leverage his connections in the underworld and in law enforcement to facilitate the needs of his clients and to maximize his own benefit. He would often find himself caught between those two worlds and could change allegiance at the drop of a hat.

In late 1869, John W. Collins, a young Boston city treasury clerk, began embezzling city funds. Collins was responsible for making payments on the city's debt and had access to large sums of money in the form of government coupons, greenbacks and gold. He started out taking small amounts, twenty-five or thirty dollars at a time, but he was using the money to gamble, and the amounts stolen increased each time as he tried to recoup his losses.

John Bull was probably the first to realize what Collins was up to. In January 1870, Bull was working a case that had him in and out of city hall, and he took notice when he recognized the young treasury clerk making large wagers at faro tables on Court Street. According to Collins, John Bull befriended him and assisted by exchanging greenbacks and bonds for hard currency and sometimes exchanging treasury gold for less conspicuous money. He gave Collins gambling advice and sometimes even placed bets for him. But Bull worried that Collins would get caught. "You are playing too publicly," Bull told him. "The gamblers want to know who you are; you must go to some quieter place."

Collins was afraid that he would be cheated if he played at quieter places, but quiet or not, he was probably being cheated wherever he played. He was on a serious losing streak and had soon lost nearly $10,000 of the treasury's money. Collins claimed that Bull suggested he alter the books to hide the loss. When Collins told him that was impossible, Bull said the only solution was to leave town as soon as possible. Collins, John Bull and Bull's girlfriend, Kitty, planned to take a train to New York City and then a steamer to Europe, traveling as "Mr. Mortimer, wife, and brother." Bull told him to steal as much as he could and then meet them at the depot. Collins stole another $1,500 in gold from the treasury and then left city hall out the back door. He had not gone far down Court Street when he felt a hand on his shoulder. Officer Wood had also seen Collins at a gambling house and started watching his movements and had gathered enough evidence to put John Collins under arrest. Collins was tried, convicted and sentenced to two and a half years in prison.

John Bull was arrested as well, on two counts of receiving stolen goods. Denying the charges, Bull said that he "acted solely as a detective in bringing out the crime and fastening it upon the right party." He admitted to making bets for Collins and had once given him $120 in greenbacks for $100 in gold. Collins, he said, admitted to him that "a prominent individual" had instructed Collins to lie about Bull. As the *National Aegis* put it, "The statements of John Bull may be taken at par, or below par, at option." Bull was released on $300 bail; his case was postponed and never reopened.

That June, John Bull was arrested again, this time for receiving stolen merchandise. Two thieves, Curtin and Cody, stole a tray full of gold chains from Fogg and Sawyer's jewelry store. They confessed to the crime and were sentenced to prison but claimed that they sold the chains to "Jew Dick" and John Bull.

The police arrested Richard Myers, alias Jew Dick, and James Donahoe, alias John Bull, and both men were released on bail pending their trial for receiving stolen merchandise. Myers immediately jumped bail and fled to Canada. Several months later, he turned up in Baltimore and was extradited back to Boston. On questioning, Myers admitted to buying the chains but said he did it at the direction of John Bull. At a later police interview with Myers, Bull, Curtin and Cody together, the story they all agreed upon was that Curtin and Cody offered to sell the chains to Bull and he declined but, seeing Myers coming down the street, said, "There is a man who is a broker and deals in such things, perhaps he will buy them." Bull made the introductions, and the transaction was done in the water closet of a building on Howard Street in the West End. At that time, Myers admitted that he had acted alone. At his trial, Myers changed his story again and tried to implicate Bull, but it was too late. Charges against John Bull were dropped, and Richard Myers was found guilty.

In July 1879, John Bull very nearly went to prison on the charge of attempting to procure "straw bail"—that is, finding someone to act as guarantor of a prisoner's bail without actually having the necessary assets. The previous November, M. Frank Paige, a drinking buddy of John Bull's in flusher times, ran into some financial difficulties. He ran a wholesale shoe business that was having difficulty meeting its expenses. At a meeting of his creditors, Paige revealed two surprising facts: first, he had a co-partner in the business, his bookkeeper, C.D. Stetson, and second, Stetson had been using company funds for personal ends and had absconded with the books to hide the amount. Paige assured his creditors that the business was not failing and he had no intention of defaulting on his debts, but for the short run, he would have to suspend payments.

It soon became clear that, whether or not Stetson was guilty or even existed, Paige was surely part of the plan and was defaulting on debts to the tune of $100,000. His creditors went after everything from his business inventory to the furniture of his home. They finally had him arrested for fraud, and his bail was set at $40,000. Paige's friends were trying to raise bail and had found a man who would guarantee half; one of his friends, Mr. Brock, offered $800 to anyone who could furnish the other half. John Bull decided to step up. He believed he could find a man to fit the bill and maybe make some money himself.

He found a man named Frank J. Watson, a drifter with nothing going for him but the fact that he was unknown to the police and anyone connected to Paige. Bull offered Watson $400 if he would impersonate a valid bondsman, Watson accepted and the charade began. He bought Watson a new suit of clothes and some false whiskers and then coached him to portray himself as an Exchange Street broker who owned unencumbered property on South Margin Street worth $30,000.

Watson offered himself up as bondsman for M. Frank Paige, but Bull's coaching had not been effective. In the bail interview, Watson gave many conflicting answers, making his claims suspect. Realizing he had botched the job, Watson took off for New York City. Brock, who had offered $800 for a bondsman, left town as well. John Bull stayed in Boston and was arrested for suborning a witness to perjury.

The trial of John Bull for suborning perjury was a sensation, overshadowing the original fraud case against Paige in press coverage. The case against Watson was clear; it was easy to prove that he was not a broker, did not own property and could not afford to guarantee $20,000 of Paige's bail. At issue was Bull's role in the perjury. He testified to telling Watson that Brock was looking for someone to put up Paige's bail but claimed that was the extent of his connection. Bull's son, his brother-in-law and two nieces testified that Bull was at the brother-in-law's house on the day he allegedly prepared Watson. After seven days of testimony, the jury failed to return a verdict; they were deadlocked, six to six. Bull was released on bail, and the case was never retried.

John Bull was clearly well connected on both sides of the law and, like Bose Cobb, had a remarkable ability to manipulate events in his favor. Cobb saw John Bull as the perfect man, in October 1885, to interview Mrs. Hamilton regarding her murder-for-hire request and to determine his best course of action. Cobb arranged a meeting between Mrs. Hamilton and John Bull, portraying himself as a man willing to take on the requested task. They met several times, and Mrs. Hamilton gradually revealed the details of her plan.

The intended victim was Mrs. Edward L. Mellen of Baltimore, Maryland, married to the son of Adrian L. Mellen, proprietor of the St. James Hotel in that city. She was born Mary A. Somerset, had come to Baltimore from England and had taken a job as a maid at the hotel, where she caught the eye of twenty-five-year-old Edward Mellen. Mellen fell in love with the bright young English girl; he seduced her, and they began to live secretly as husband and wife under the names Mr. and Mrs. Edward Lester. Before long, Mary was pregnant.

In April 1885, nine months after the birth of their child, Mary and Edward had a disagreement, and Mary went to

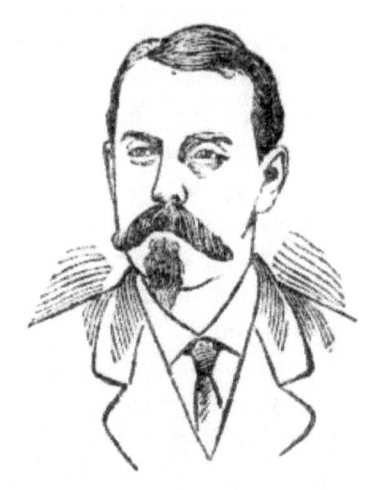

Adrian L. Mellen. *From* Boston Post, *March 17, 1886.*

Edward's father to make him aware of her situation and introduce him to his grandchild. Mr. Mellen was horrified and insisted that the couple marry immediately, and they agreed. Edward's mother was not told of the marriage, and his father never accepted his daughter-in-law, believing that his son had married beneath his station. In fact, he was so put out that Adrian Mellen told Mrs. Hamilton that he was willing to do whatever was necessary to "remove" the low-class girl from the family.

Mrs. Hamilton told Bull that she had tried twice to poison the girl but realized she was not up to the job of murder and decided to find someone else to do it. She was familiar with Bose Cobb and thought that he could discreetly find her someone to do the job. John Bull told her he would go to Baltimore and arrange the murder of Mary Mellen, and his last meeting with Mrs. Hamilton was taken up with negotiating the price and settling the details. On Friday, October 23, 1885, John Bull was to go to the Revere House and pick up an envelope containing ten $100 bills. Then on Saturday, they would go to the telegraph office and wire Mellen that the plan was in motion.

John Bull took all the information back to Bose Cobb, and both men agreed that the best course of action was to take the story to the police. On Saturday night, October 24, 1885, Police Inspector Geraughty followed John Bull as he and Mrs. Hamilton went to the telegraph office. Inspector

Houghton was already there, masquerading as the telegraph operator. Mrs. Hamilton handed him this message:

Oct. 24, 1885
To Adrian L. Mellen, St. James Hotel Baltimore Md.: Rooms rented opposite to house. Work to be done Monday sure. Send party away, without fail, as before. Send me word when to have money paid. We want those papers they have J.E.C.

She was immediately placed under arrest. Following her arrest, the woman's true identity was made known: she was Mrs. Emma Coolidge, wife of Boston police officer James E. Coolidge. But it had not been a police sting; Officer Coolidge was as surprised as anyone that his wife had been attempting to arrange a murder in Baltimore.

Mrs. Coolidge was interrogated in a hotel room, away from the prying eyes of the press. Inspectors Geraughty and Houghton, accompanied by John Bull, left Boston by train, ostensibly for Washington, D.C., but they were going to Baltimore. Beyond what was already known, the police were not giving reporters further information on the details of the case or the plans of the police officers pursuing it.

After several days with no new information from the police, the papers began to weave their stories based on the facts they had and on the reputations of John Bull and Bose Cobb. On October 29, the *Boston Herald* speculated that the whole affair had been a botched blackmail scheme. Their theory was that Emma Coolidge and John Bull had planned to "deliberately bleed a sorrow-stricken family." Mrs. Coolidge, who knew the Mellen family secrets, conspired with John Bull to put the pinch on Mr. Mellen by threatening to charge him with planning to murder an objectionable daughter-in-law, thereby exposing his son's low-class bride and their bastard child, jeopardizing his career and his standing in society. Bose Cobb got wind of the affair and, to curry favor with the new police board, told the story to the commissioners. But Bull suspected Cobb's

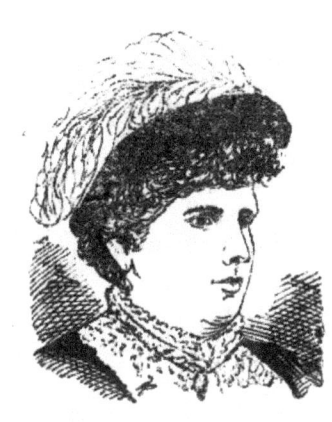

Mrs. Emma Coolidge. *From* Boston Post, *March 17, 1886.*

plan, and while Cobb was meeting with the commissioners, Bull took the story to police headquarters, giving up Mrs. Coolidge and, as he often did, posing as an agent of justice. The *Herald*'s story was picked up by a number of newspapers across the country.

Speculation faded away as news from Baltimore began to arrive in Boston that the inspectors were definitely there to arrest Adrian Mellen. They had trouble locating him and finally learned that he was staying at the Colonnade Hotel in Philadelphia. He issued a statement calling Mrs. Coolidge a crank, saying she must be crazy. He admitted to meeting her but said they were not close and she had no connection to his son Edward. Edward Mellen took the whole affair as a joke and said there was no trouble between his father and himself and he had no idea who Mrs. Coolidge was. The inspectors returned to Boston empty-handed.

In November, Mellen returned to Baltimore and was staying in a room in the St. James Hotel, refusing to see anyone. The Boston officers also returned to Baltimore, this time armed with an indictment and extradition papers from the governor of Massachusetts. But the papers were not served because Mellen's attorneys were preparing to have the Boston officers arrested on a countercharge of conspiracy against Mellen. Baltimore police said they would not arrest Mellen until the governor of Maryland issued an affirmative response to the requisition. While this standoff transpired, Adrian Mellen quietly slipped out of town, bound for parts unknown.

In March 1886, any doubts about the story disappeared when Mrs. Emma Coolidge pleaded guilty to the charge of conspiracy to commit murder and was sentenced to three years in the women's reformatory prison in Sherborn, Massachusetts. Outside of court, she told reporters that she thought a great deal of Adrian Mellen and would do anything for him. She had met him in New York City before she met and married Officer Coolidge. She would not state what her relations with Mellen were, but they must have been well acquainted for him to contact her regarding the murder of his daughter-in-law. Officer Coolidge was deeply humiliated by his wife's behavior and stated the only course for him was to sell the house and move west with their little daughter.

Adrian Mellen was finally located in Topo Chico, Mexico. The Boston authorities determined that conspiracy to commit murder was not a crime for which Mexico would arrest and extradite Mellen, but they intended to have the border watched and have him arrested if he should cross. Mellen was adjusting to his new life in Mexico, and it was reported that he was trying to obtain a $10,000 loan to open a hotel in Monterey.

Chapter 15

THE END OF AN ERA

$\mathcal{B}$ose Cobb finally made good on his plan to leave the West End. After another raid in January 1886, the dance hall that he had nominally given up a year earlier closed for good, and he moved his center of operations to Brighton, far from the West End but still within Boston city limits. He planned to change the nature of his operations as well, opening the Charles River Hotel on North Harvard Street and Warren Avenue, which would feature a "temperance café," serving no intoxicants at all. Cobb informed the police that he meant "to conduct himself in the future as a good citizen should." But that June, he applied for a liquor license for another establishment in Berry's Corner, Brighton—a dance hall, saloon and brothel. Police in Brighton, so far from the heart of town, were not greatly affected by the reorganization and were, no doubt, happy to look the other way for a price.

At the end of 1887, Bose Cobb fell into a serious streak of bad luck. That December, sparks from the stove ignited a fire in his apartment on Fay Street in the South End, forcing him to move his residence to Berry's Corner. In June 1888, a freak tornado touched down in Brighton. The storm occurred around 10:00 p.m., so the normally crowded streets were empty, and there were no fatalities, but stores and factories sustained extensive damage. A portion of the roof of the Charles River Hotel was ripped off, and the hotel's chimney "snapped like a pipe stem." The dance hall was damaged as well.

Pneumonia laid Cobb low the following February, leaving him bedridden for three months. In early May, he felt strong enough to leave the house and venture into the city, but when he returned home, he relapsed. On May 11, 1889, Bose Cobb died of heart failure.

Emory Boardman Cobb was buried in his hometown of Natick, Massachusetts. The "simple but impressive" services were held at the home of a relative, conducted by the minister of the Congregational Orthodox church. Long before the services began, a large crowd of people from Boston and elsewhere gathered in and around the house to pay their respects. "Jumping Jim" Henderson and other Boston associates of Bose Cobb joined his brothers as pallbearers.

Estimates varied as to the size of Bose Cobb's estate. His ventures had generated large sums of money over the years, but Cobb had extravagant tastes and spent heavily on police bribes to keep the dance hall open and to stay informed on police raids. He had been married at least three times and had several young children, but his favorite was always his daughter Nellie, sixteen years old at the time of his death. Nellie inherited whatever was left of Cobb's fortune. At the funeral, she placed on his coffin a beautiful cross of roses and lilies bearing the inscription in immortelles "Papa."

Newspapers in Boston and throughout the country memorialized the death of Bose Cobb, retelling the story of his criminal career under headlines such as "Boston Loses a Very Wicked Man" and "One of Boston's Bad Men Gone to Settle His Account." But before long, the papers began to reassess the Wickedest Man in Boston. A story titled "Not So Bad After All" in the *New Haven Register* stated that those who were acquainted with Bose Cobb knew he was not nearly as bad as the newspapers made him. They quoted one well-known sporting man:

> *Bose was dark enough in all truth, but somebody managed to paint him a little blacker. Did you ever stop to think that the police might have closed Cobb's sporting career long, long ago? And did you ever ask yourself why they didn't do it? No, my boy; this black villain had money to give away that was always one color, and that was genuine yellow, no matter whose hand it passed through. It is a strange fact, also that this desperate scoundrel was leeway on the side of law and order; and if he had done as a police officer what he did gratuitously as a common citizen to prevent crime and to capture criminals, his record would be pointed to as a model for every ambitious member of the force. It is an undisputed fact that Cobb never harbored a criminal and never countenanced crime. He used to say that the people who came into his place came there to the safety of public life and property. They were all hardened creatures and none of them had ever come*

to his place until they had become hardened. If they had remained out of his resort, they would have gone somewhere else where they'd have done more damage....At one time he had money, but he had to give it all away, and he became, in fact, whatever he was in name, an agent of the police. "Bose" Cobb wasn't a saint, but if he was a devil, he paid high license.

Other writers waxed nostalgic with a nagging sense that the death of Bose Cobb marked the end of an era in Boston. One by one the old saloons, dance halls and theaters were closing their doors. Gone were the days when a policeman would ignore an unlicensed grogshop, turn a blind eye to a peaceful faro bank or wait for a formal complaint to shut down a house of ill fame. For better or worse, the "free and easy" attitude that characterized the earlier decades of Victorian Boston was gone forever.

Some of the era's most notorious characters would not live to see its end. Barney Ford, the owner of the North End rat pit, entered Tom Kiley's North Street dancing saloon at about 3:00 a.m. one Sunday morning in 1862. Seeing an acquaintance, Michael A. Sullivan, he asked Mr. Sullivan if he would not have a drink with him. Sullivan declined, and Ford commenced to abusing him in a most foul-mouthed manner, the level of insult and threat of violence increasing until Ford promised he would kill Sullivan before the night was over. Sullivan did his best to ignore the threats until Ford forced him into a corner, drew a knife and stabbed him in the gut. Sullivan then drew his knife and stabbed Ford between the ribs, in the abdomen and in other vital parts. Barney Ford was dead in ten minutes.

As the public continued to speculate on the identity of the characters in Reverend Henry Morgan's *Boston Inside Out!*, it came out that the lecherous priest Father Titus was, in reality, the Very Reverend Patrick F. Lyndon, vicar general of the Archdiocese of Boston, and the real name of his "niece," Rose Delaney, was Frances V. Keefe. Mrs. Keefe sued Morgan for libel, asking $25,000 in damages, for insinuating that she had committed the crime of adultery. Morgan produced a document, written by her husband, Joseph P. Keefe, recounting in intimate detail the relationship between Francis Keefe and Father Lyndon. The case promised to become a major scandal, but Henry Morgan, whose health had never been sound, died of pneumonia at age fifty-nine before the case could be tried.

John L. Sullivan successfully defended the World Heavyweight Championship for ten years before being knocked out in 1892 by Gentleman Jim Corbett. Following his defeat, Sullivan's health began to fail. Years of overeating and alcohol abuse took their toll, leaving him overweight and dissipated. Sullivan finally gave up drinking and went on the lecture circuit speaking against alcohol, but temperance lectures did not pay as well as prize fights, and he died a pauper in 1918 at age fifty-nine.

Reverend William Downs's legal dispute against the Bowdoin Square Baptist Church continued for several more years until he finally won a lawsuit awarding him $10,000 in damages. The split in the Bowdoin Square Baptist Church due to the Taber/Downs case resulted in the demise of one of the city's oldest Baptist congregations. The church itself was sold in 1916 to the New England Telephone and Telegraph Company, which demolished it to build its headquarters.

Elmer Chickering's brief dabbling in obscene photography did not hamper his career. He expanded his portrait work to include champion sports figures, politicians and famous actors and actresses. He photographed Princess Kaiulani of Hawaii and President William McKinley, and his pictures appeared in magazines such as *Good Housekeeping*. If he retained any traces of the objectionable photographs of Boston debutants, they were destroyed in a studio fire in 1903 along with hundreds of Chickering's negatives.

By the end of the nineteenth century, Boston's police force, which had been so reluctant to hire an Irishman, was dominated by Irish officers. Police positions were plum jobs to be doled out by the city administration, now dominated by Irish politicians. They ruled, not in a Tammany-style machine, as the Know-Nothings feared, but in ward-based fiefdoms, rife with feuds and vengeance, setting the tone of Boston politics into the next century. They were led by colorful figures such as "Dapper" Dan Coakley, Martin "Mahatma" Lomasney and the grandfathers of President John F. Kennedy, John "Honey Fitz" Fitzgerald and Patrick "P.J." Kennedy.

"Chicken" Welch's life of crime ended abruptly in 1901 when he and a friend, Timothy Coughran, decided to leave Boston and tour the southern states. They left Back Bay riding on top of a freight car. The travelers had not even left the city when the train went under a low bridge that neither had seen. Coughran was killed instantly, and Welch was thrown from the car, sustaining spine injuries that left him crippled for the rest of his life.

Warry S. Charles, the Chinese interpreter brought from New York to help with the "Wash-House Murder," remained in Boston and became one of the richest men in Chinatown. By the turn of the century, the Chinese "companies" were known as tongs in Boston, as they were in the rest of the country, and had been reduced to two: Hep Sing and On Leong. Warry Charles rose to become the leader of the Hep Sing tong, which specialized

Invading Highbinders on Murder Raid In Chinatown Kill Three---Seven More May Die in War of Secret Societies

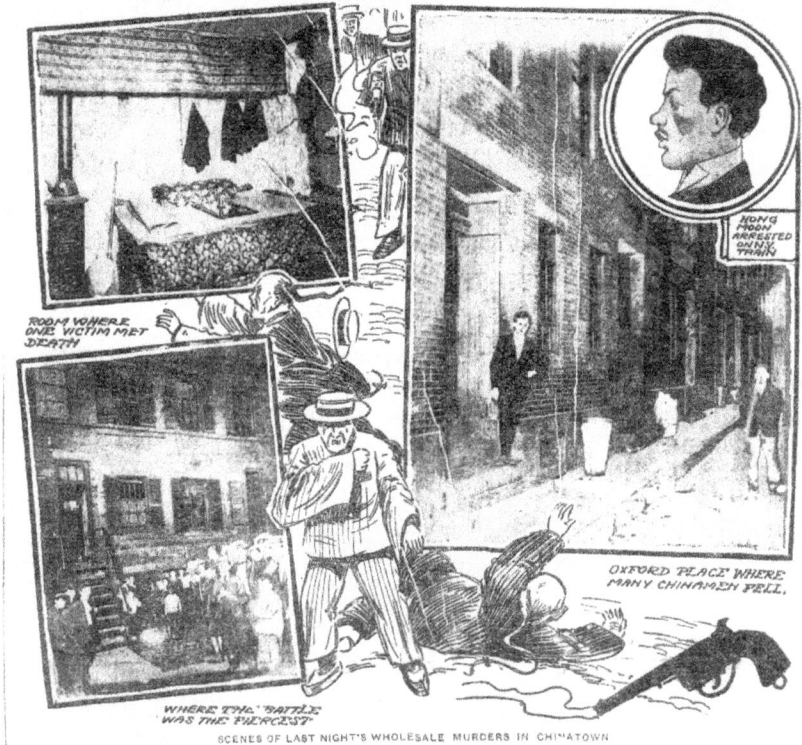

Invading highbinders. *From* Boston Post, *August 3, 1907.*

in gambling and extortion. To end their long feud with On Leong and to frighten honest Chinese businessmen into joining their organization, Charles proposed that Hep Sing murder the leaders of On Leong. On the night of August 2, 1907, "highbinders" from out of town, armed with hatchets and army revolvers, wreaked havoc in Chinatown, leaving four dead and six wounded. The following May, Warry Charles and seven others were found guilty of first-degree murder.

Adrian Mellen, who had fled the country to avoid prosecution for arranging the murder of his daughter-in-law, was last seen in Topo Chico, Mexico. Though he appeared to be thriving there, planning to build a hotel, he did not remain in Mexico long. He made his way to Canada and lived in Toronto until November 1893, when he died of pneumonia. His body was brought back to the United States, and he was buried in the city of his birth, Cambridge, Massachusetts.

In 1891, the New England Society for the Suppression of Vice officially changed its name to the Watch and Ward Society, the name taken from the Puritan "watch and ward," a group of citizens chosen by lot to assist the constable in warding off evildoers. The success the group had in passing legislation empowering officers to make arrests based on the mere presence of gambling equipment, together with more energetic enforcement due to the police reorganization, had the effect of driving gambling further underground, if not fully eliminating it. Some of the larger gambling houses took out charters as private clubs, giving them the status of literary and social clubs and protecting them from arrest for gambling as long as everyone present was a member of the club. This set off another round of legislative lobbying.

The Watch and Ward Society finally succeeded in restoring the small but essential word "or" to the state statute regarding obscene literature. The statute now banned any work that was "obscene, immoral, and impure or manifestly tending to corrupt the morals of youth," giving it tremendous leverage in the fight against demoralizing literature. The society prosecuted modern writers such as H.L. Mencken for profanity and objectionable subject matter, as well as continuing to prohibit the sale of unacceptable classics. This crusade was so successful that "banned in Boston" became a catchphrase in the twentieth century, describing any racy literature.

The Howard Theater outlasted everyone, serving up burlesque to generations of college students, servicemen on leave, politicians and Boston gentlemen of every class in the center of Scollay Square, Boston's vice district for most of the twentieth century. When the Old Howard was demolished for urban renewal in the 1960s along with Scollay Square and much of the West End, Boston vice slithered down to Washington Street, finding a new home as the Combat Zone. The Combat Zone disappeared as well when the Internet made strip clubs, peep shows and adult bookstores superfluous.

The success of temperance societies in Boston and elsewhere in the country passing the Eighteenth Amendment, prohibiting alcohol, ushered in a new age of organized crime and bloody gang wars, which may ebb and flow but will never go away. The petty crime of the free-and-easies in Boston seems quaint by comparison. It is easy to ignore the sins and paint with a rosy brush the simple pleasures of Boston's wicked Victorian era, but for better or worse, those days are gone forever.

SOURCES

1. Sins of a Great City

Boston Daily Globe. "Shot by His Companion." August 7, 1885.

Boston Sunday Globe. "Was It Accidental?" August 9, 1885.

Daily Atlas. "[Boston; Ann Street; Milk Street; Boston]." June 19, 1845.

Morgan, Henry, PMP. *Ned Nevins, the News Boy*. Boston: Lee and Shepard, 1867.

Morgan, Rev. Henry. *Boston Inside Out!* Boston: Shawmut Publishing Company, 1883.

———. *Shadowy Hand*. Boston: Morgan Chapel, 1874.

Seventh Annual Report of the N.E. Society for the Suppression of Vice. Boston: Deland & Barta, 1885.

Steen, Ivan D. "Cleansing the Puritan City: The Reverend Henry Morgan's Antivice Crusade in Boston." *New England Quarterly* (September 1, 1981): 385.

2. The Black Sea

American Traveler. "Reform in Ann Street." February 13, 1851.

Boston Daily Bee. "Annual Report of the Police Department." January 25, 1851.

———. "Dance Cellar." October 24, 1846.

———. "Stella Lea, the Orphan Girl." September 21, 1846.

———. "Violation of the License Law." April 19, 1843.

———. "Violators of the Sunday Law." October 20, 1846.

Boston Evening Transcript. "Life in Ann Street." January 7, 1851.

———. "Police Descent in Ann Street." April 24, 1851.

Boston Herald. "Another Descent of Police." April 24, 1851.

———. "Crime in Boston." January 14, 1851.

———. "Mrs. Anna Cooley." March 23, 1861.

———. "The Reform Mission in North Street." June 1, 1860.

———. "Street Preaching." August 20, 1853.

Boston Recorder. "Letter from Philadelphia." April 29, 1858.

———. "North Street Independent Mission." June 2, 1859.

———. "Police Descent in Ann Street." May 1, 1851.

———. "Rev. Perez Mason." March 19, 1857.

Boston Traveler. "Carrying the War into Africa." February 9, 1858.

———. "Oak Hall." September 23, 1842.

Gloucester Telegraph. "Riot in Ann Street." August 30, 1843.

Goldfeld, Alex R. *The North End.* Charleston, SC: The History Press, 2009.

Hampshire Gazette. "Riot in Boston." August 29, 1843.

National Aegis. "Singular Affair in Boston." January 29, 1851.

Newburyport Herald. "[Goddard; Estate; Recently; Auction; Mr. Carney; Boston; Business; Mentioned]." April 27, 1843.

Savage, Edward Hartwell. *Police Records and Recollections.* Boston: John P. Dale & Company, 1873.

Washington Reporter. "A City Missionary 'Sentenced.'" February 11, 1857.

Weekly Messenger. "Descent on Ann Street." April 30, 1851.

———. "The Late Affray in Ann Street." August 30, 1843.

3. Baiting Rats and Bucking the Tiger

Annual Report of the N.E. Society for the Suppression of Vice for the Year 1885. Boston: Deland & Bart, 1885.

Annual Report of the N.E. Society for the Suppression of Vice for the Year 1889. Boston: Office of the Society, 1889)

Boston Daily Advertiser. "Adolph Albrecht." June 27, 1888.

———. "Good Work Well Done." May 7, 1885.

Boston Daily Globe. "Pool Selling Defined." October 19, 1889.

Boston Herald. "Albrecht Arraigned." March 30, 1887.

———. "Albrecht at the Bar." April 23, 1887.

———. "The Gambling Hell." November 2, 1885.

———. "Raid on Gamblers." November 27, 1885.

Boston Journal. "Albrecht Indicted." June 10, 1887.

———. "The Avery Street Tragedy." April 15, 1887.

———. "Gamblers Shot Down." March 29, 1887.

———. "The Gambling House Tragedy." March 29, 1887.

Boston Traveler. "'Rare Sport' at the West End." April 29, 1870.

Macon Telegraph. "A 'Brace' Game." March 29, 1887.

Morgan, Rev. Henry. *Boston Inside Out!* Boston: Shawmut Publishing Company, 1883.

New York Herald. "Homicide over Cards." March 29, 1887.

———. "The Tiger in Boston." April 1, 1887.

Savage, Edward Hartwell. *Police Records and Recollections.* Boston: John P. Dale & Company, 1873.

4. The Guilty Third Tier

Beecher, Henry Ward. *Lectures to Young Men on Various Important Subjects.* New York: J.C. Derby, 1856.

Boston Commercial Gazette. "[Major Noah; Jack Reeve; Adelphitheatre; London; Park; Major; Allowance; Representation]." December 7, 1835.

Boston Daily Bee. "The Corner Stone of the Howard Athenaeum." July 6, 1846.

———. "Police Court." March 22, 1843.

———. "Police Court." November 23, 1844.

Boston Evening Transcript. "Hearing on the Question of Imposing Additional Restrictions on Theatres." September 4, 1846.

———. "Howard Athenæum." July 3, 1846.

———. "The Howard Athenæum." September 24, 1846.

Boston Post. "Cheap Amusements." January 15, 1841.

———. "Proprietors of the Tremont Theatre." May 25, 1841.

Christian Watchman. "Tremont Temple." December 8, 1843.

Eastern Argus. "[Jack Reeve; New York; Major Noah; Cockneys; Loco Focos]." December 9, 1835.

Engle, Ron. *The American Stage.* Cambridge, UK: Cambridge University Press, 1993.

Hampshire Gazette. "[Tremont Temple; Purchased; Boston; Dedicated; God]." December 12, 1843.

Johnson, Claudia Durst. *Church and Stage*. Jefferson, NC: MacFarland & Company, Inc., 2008.

———. "That Guilty Third Tier: Prostitution in Nineteenth-Century American Theaters." *American Quarterly* (December 1975): 575.

Kruh, David. *Always Something Doing*. Boston: Faber and Faber, 1990.

Logan, Olive. *Before the Footlights and Behind the Scenes*. Philadelphia: Parmelee & Co., 1870.

Morgan, Rev. Henry. *Boston Inside Out!* Boston: Shawmut Publishing Company, 1883.

Newark Daily Advertiser. September 17, 1846.

Public Ledger. "Deadly Weapons." March 18, 1837.

———. "Judicial Decision." March 17, 1840.

5. Obscenity

Annual Report of the N.E. Society for the Suppression of Vice, for the Year 1883. Boston: Alfred Mudge & Son, 1883.

Annual Report of the N.E. Society for the Suppression of Vice, for the Year 1886. Boston: Alfred Mudge & Son, 1886.

Arkansas Gazette. "Fair Damsels Have Pictures Taken in a Nude State, and Cause Trouble." June 12, 1887.

Beisel, Nicola Kay. *Imperiled Innocents*. Princeton, NJ: Princeton University Press, 1998.

Boston Daily Globe. "Are the Pictures Obscene?" November 22, 1887.

———. "Elmer Chickering in Court." June 11, 1887.

———. "Is the Word Obscene?" May 24, 1890.

———. "Two Years for Heywood." July 24, 1890.

Censorpedia. "Cupid's Yokes (pamphlet)." wiki.ncac.org.

Columbus Daily Enquirer. "As Greek Goddesses." June 14, 1887.

Dallas Morning News. "Art Devotees." June 12, 1887.

Editors' Notes. "Ezra Heywood's Obscenity Trial for Cupid's Yolk." editorsnotes.org.

Elkhart Daily Review. "A Boston Photographer in Trouble." June 8, 1887.

Fort Worth Daily Gazette. "Boston's Fair Ones." July 26, 1887.

Gordon, Linda. *The Moral Property of Women*. Chicago: University of Illinois Press, 2002.

Historic Camera. "Elmer Chickering." historiccamera.com.

Miller, Neil. *Banned in Boston*. Boston: Beacon Press, 2010.

Mitchell Daily Republican. "The Human Form Divine." July 21, 1887.
National Police Gazette. "Nine Naughty Young Girls." December 2, 1882.
New York Herald. "Too Too High Art." June 7, 1887.
New York Times. "A Rash Photographer." June 11, 1887.
Pittsburgh Daily Post. "Boston Is Shocked." June 11, 1887.
Saint Paul Globe. "Giddy Girls of Boston." June 11, 1887.
St. Louis Post-Dispatch. "Devotees of True Art." June 7, 1887.
Topeka Daily Capital. "Cultured Boston's Latest Sensation." June 12, 1887.
Wichita Beacon. "The Nude at the Hub." June 11, 1887.

6. The Social Evil

Biddeford Daily Journal. "Julia Hilton's Will." November 18, 1885.
Boston City Directory, 1882. Boston. 1882.
Boston Daily Globe. "Back from His Trip." July 10, 1885.
———. "Board of Police Commissioners." April 18, 1883.
———. "For Keeping a Bagnio." November 7, 1885.
———. "Found Caged." November 5, 1885.
———. "Sale of the Glen Hotel." June 6, 1890.
Boston Herald. "Alleged Brutal Treatment." November 7, 1885.
Boston Journal. "Real Estate." February 5, 1883.
———. "The Sanborn Will Case." January 1, 1886.
———. "Two Wills to Be Contested." September 21, 1885.
Boston Post. "Real Estate Transfers." December 9, 1887.
———. "Suffolk County Real Estate Attachments." January 27, 1885.
Cleveland Leader. "A Dual Life." September 21, 1885.
Daily Inter Ocean. "For Woman's Honor." January 23, 1886.
Evansville Courier and Press. "All This in Civilized Boston." November 6, 1885.
Find a Grave. "Maj Edward Stevens Sanborn." www.findagrave.com.
Lowell Daily Courier. "Will Case Compromised." November 19, 1885.
Morgan, Rev. Henry. *Boston Inside Out!* Boston: Shawmut Publishing Company, 1883.
National Police Gazette. "Boston Brutality." November 21, 1885.
———. "A Double Life." October 10, 1885.
New York Times. "Dartmouth Interested in a Will." September 13, 1885.
———. "The Sanborn Will Probated." February 24, 1886.
Plain Dealer. "Found Naked." November 7, 1885.
Springfield Republican. "E. Sanborn's Double Life." September 21, 1885.

———. "The Sanborn Will Case." September 21, 1885.

Steen, Ivan D. "Cleansing the Puritan City: The Reverend Henry Morgan's Antivice Crusade in Boston." *New England Quarterly* (September 1, 1981).

7. Confidence

Boston Daily Globe. "Buying Gold Bricks." December 28, 1882.

———. "On the Old Charge." September 27, 1883.

Boston Herald. "The Banco Swindle." May 25, 1882.

———. "Beating a Statesman." April 7, 1882.

———. "Errors and Evil." December 28, 1882.

———. "Noted Swindler Dead." May 18, 1886.

———. "The Ring Racket." February 20, 1883.

———. "They Don't Understand." April 9, 1882.

———. "The Wildcat Prize." April 9, 1882.

Boston Post. "The Dark Side of Life." December 28, 1882.

Byrnes, Thomas. *Professional Criminals of America.* New York: Castle & Company, Ltd., 1886.

Critic-Record (Washington, D.C.). "One Bunco Man Less." November 3, 1885.

Defenders and Offenders. New York: D. Buchner & Co., 1888.

Eldridge, Benjamin P., and William B. Watts. *Our Rival, the Rascal: A Faithful Portrayal of the Conflict between the Criminals of This Age and the Defenders of Society, the Police.* Boston: Pemberton Pub. Co., 1896.

National Police Gazette. "Joseph Eaton." January 27, 1883.

———. "A New Confidence Man Caught." December 16, 1882.

———. "William Baker." December 26, 1882.

New York Daily Graphic, April 8, 1882.

New York Herald. "Banished from Boston." December 29, 1882.

———. "The Boston Sensation." April 8, 1882.

———. "City News Items." May 17, 1883.

New York Times. "Mr. C.F. Adams's Troubles." May 25, 1882.

Savage, Edward Hartwell. *Police Records and Recollections.* Boston: John P. Dale & Company, 1873.

8. Fresh from the Bogs

Boston Daily Globe. "'Chicken' Welch in Trouble." May 21, 1896.

———. "'Chicken' Welch Showed Fight." December 17, 1896.

———. "South Boston." June 25, 1894.

———. "Through Prison Walls." April 18, 1885.

Boston Herald. "'The Chicken' Arrested." January 22, 1898.

———. "Municipal Court—Judge Parmenter." September 4, 1879.

———. "South Boston." December 7, 1881.

———. "Superior Civil Court—Third Session." April 26, 1879.

———. "Superior Criminal Court." October 18, 1882.

Boston Journal. "'Chicken' to Be Cooped." January 22, 1895.

———. "'Chicken Welch' Again." May 21, 1896.

———. "'Chicken' Welch Nabbed." April 24, 1885.

———. "Escaped from State Prison." April 18, 1885.

Boston Post. "'Chicken' Welch Caught." May 21, 1896.

Evening Star. "Prisoners in Rebellion." August 8, 1890.

Gleason's Pictorial Drawing-Room Companion. "Henry J. Gardner Esq." December 2, 1854.

Lane, Roger. *Policing the City.* New York: Athenaeum, 1975.

Mulkern, John R. *The Know-Nothing Party in Massachusetts.* Boston: Northeastern University Press, 1990.

New Haven Register. "Gov. Russel Pardons Chicken Welch." March 18, 1892.

———. "Through the Ventilator." April 18, 1885.

New York Herald. "Fire in a Prison." May 9, 1885.

O'Neill, Gerard. *Rogues and Redeemers.* New York: Crown Publishers, 2012.

Puleo, Stephen. *A City So Grand: The Rise of an American Metropolis: Boston 1850–1900.* Boston: Beacon Press, 2010.

Stevens, Peter F. *Hidden History of the Boston Irish.* Charleston, SC: The History Press, 2008.

9. Chinatown

Boston Daily Advertiser "Chinamen in Custody." October 5, 1885.

———. "A Local Opium Joint." April 4, 1885.

———. "Opium and Chinaman: How Both Are Smuggled into the Country in Spite of Laws." October 30, 1889.

———. "Our Chinese Neighbors." March 16, 1886.

Boston Daily Globe. "Ding Chong's Murder." July 21, 1886.

———. "Influx of Chinese." March 13, 1884.

———. "Looking Up Clews." July 20, 1886.

————. "The Police at Bay." July 22, 1886.

————. "Yee Gow the Man." September 14, 1886.

Boston Herald. "Chinese." March 15, 1886.

————. "Crisp and Casual." October 1, 1886.

————. "Lively Times in Chinatown." July 14, 1890.

————. "Not a Word from the Johns." July 22, 1886.

————. "Sam Lung's 'Joint.'" January 29, 1885.

————. "Saw Him Get into a Herdic." July 20, 1886.

————. "They Will Assist." July 25, 1886

————. "Three Chinese Suspects." July 24, 1886.

————. "The Wash-House Murder." July 21, 1886.

————. "What Joe Swen Thinks." July 27, 1886.

Boston Journal. "Bin Chong Murdered." July 19, 1886.

————. "The Chinese Murder." July 26, 1886.

————. "The Chinese Tragedy." July 20, 1886.

————. "Washington Topics." April 11, 1882.

Boston Post. "The Opium Pipe." February 6, 1882.

————. "A Shocking Murder." July 19, 1886.

New York Herald. "Chinaman Cut to Pieces." July 19, 1886.

————. "Defending the Chinese." May 23, 1886.

Springfield Republican. "'Respectable' People in an Opium Joint." November 26, 1883.

10. The Sporting Life

Boston Daily Globe. "Sequel of the Great Walk." November 9, 1886.

————. "Where the Money Went." November 9, 1886.

Boston Herald. "Go-As-You-Please Contest." October 31, 1886.

————. "Go-As-You Please Match." November 2, 1886.

————. "John L Is 'Dead Broke.'" October 14, 1889.

————. "John L. Sullivan in 'Quod.'" July 29, 1882.

————. "Rink Pedestrianism." November 5, 1886.

————. "Riotous Scenes." July 3, 1885.

————. "Sporting Miscellany." November 28, 1886.

————. "Sullivan 'Lushing' Again." March 11, 1889.

————. "Sullivan's Saloon." August 9, 1883.

————. "Sullivan's Soiree." August 8, 1883.

————. "Troubles of the 'Peds.'" November 10, 1886.

Boston Journal. "John L. Sullivan under Arrest." September 14, 1885.

Boston Sunday Globe. "Guerrero Wins." November 7, 1886.

———. "Peter Golden's Benefit." November 14, 1886.

———. "To Tramp Six Days." October 31, 1886.

Cleveland Leader. "Sporting Gossip." November 8, 1883.

Daily Critic. "Sullivan's Latest Debauch." January 24, 1885.

John L. Sullivan, Champion Pugilist of the World. Michele and Donald D'amour Museum of Fine Arts, Springfield, Massachusetts. Gift of Lenore B. and Sidney A. Alpert, supplemented with Museum Acquisition Funds Photography by David Stansbury.

Klein, Christopher. *Strong Boy*. Guilford, CT: Lyons Press, 2013.

New Haven Register. "Sullivan Breaks His Pledge." October 13, 1883.

New York Herald. "John L. Sullivan's Escapades." January 12, 1885.

———. "Pugilist Sullivan Sentenced." April 27, 1882.

Patriot. "Sullivan on the Rampage." January 24, 1885.

Plain Dealer. "Ped Hart's Little Game." November 10, 1886.

Springfield Republican. "Eastern Massachusetts." November 11, 1886.

Times-Picayune. "[Mr. Richard K. Fox; New York; London; Boston; John L. Sullivan; England]." May 6, 1882.

Truth. "[Boston; Society; Hon. John L. Sullivan; Craft; Soft]." July 16, 1882.

11. Scandal

Boston Daily Advertiser. "The Downs-Taber Case." October 14, 1885.

———. "Locked Out." November 23, 1885.

Boston Daily Globe. "Booked at Station 3." August 18, 1885.

———. "Parson Downs." August 20, 1885.

———. "Watchers at No. 7." August 18, 1885.

———. "When a Maiden." August 29, 1885.

Boston Herald. "Asked to Resign." October 21, 1885.

———. "Court Record." November 12, 1885.

———. "The Latest Scandal." August 26, 1885.

———. "Mr. Downs on the Stand." December 10, 1887.

———. "Mr. Taber Expelled." September 5, 1885.

———. "Mr. Taber Wins His Case." November 10, 1885.

———. "A Muscular Christian." March 2, 1886.

———. "Near the Old Quarters." July 25, 1888.

———. "Parson Downs' Lawsuit." December 15, 1887.

———. "Peculiar Pastime Indulged in by the Husband." November 13, 1885.

———. "Rev. Mr. Downs's Salary Suit." January 6, 1887.

Boston Journal. "A Divorce Granted Mr. Taber." November 10, 1885.

———. "The Grand Jury. the Rev. Mr. Dawns and Mrs. Taber Indicted but Not Arraigned." December 12, 1885.

———. "The Mirror and the Cane." October 30, 1885.

———. "Mr. Downs and Mrs. Taber Arraigned." December 14, 1885.

———. "Recognized as Pastor." October 20, 1880.

———. "Rev. Mr. Downs and the Bowdoin Square Church." November 6, 1885.

———. "The Taber Divorce Case." November 3, 1885.

Boston Post. "The Sequel." August 19, 1885.

Cleveland Leader. "A Brutal Wretch." November 12, 1885.

Dallas Morning News. "Another Church Scandal in Boston." August 8, 1886.

———. "Rev. Mr. Downs in Another Scandal." July 13, 1886.

Evening Star. "Sequel of the Downs Scandal." August 16, 1886.

Grand Forks Daily Herald. "Much Abused Woman." November 12, 1885.

Kansas City Star. "Another Boston Sensation." November 12, 1885.

National Police Gazette. "All Broken Up." November 21, 1885.

———. "Boston High Life." November 28, 1885.

———. "'Do You Know This Towel?'" October 31, 1885.

———. "'For the Sake of Religion.'" November 14, 1885.

———. "Hub as a Moral Scenter." November 14, 1885.

———. "Loud Divorce." November 28, 1885.

———. "Parson Downs and Mrs. Taber at the Bar." January 2, 1886.

———. "Parson Downs on Trial." December 24, 1887.

———. "Taber vs Downs." November 7, 1885.

———. "They Stood by Parson Downs." December 26, 1885.

New Haven Register. "The Downs-Taber Case Nolled." December 11, 1886.

———. "Mrs. Loud Wins Her Case." November 17, 1885.

New York Herald. "Among the Puritans." May 23, 1886.

———. "Dominie Downs' Downfall." September 16, 1886.

———. "Downs and Mrs. Taber Arraigned." December 15, 1885.

———. "In Favor of Parson Downs." October 8, 1886.

———. "Mrs. Louds Divorce Suit." November 13, 1885.

———. "Parson Downs Defeated Again." June 23, 1886.

———. "Sensational New England." July 11, 1886.

———. "The Taber Divorce Confirmed." May 30, 1886.

New York Times. "Boston's Great Scandal." October 29, 1885.

———. "Butler for Pastor Downs." December 21, 1886.

———. "Parson Downs's Revenge." August 7, 1886.

New York Tribune. "Pastor Downs in Haste to Be Tried." February 9, 1886.

———. "Testimony of the Rev. W.W. Downs." October 19, 1885.

———. "Why Mr. Taber Wants a Divorce." October 27, 1885.

New York World. "Wife and Pastor in Jail." August 19, 1885.

Patriot. "Downs' New Trouble." July 12, 1886.

San Francisco Chronicle. "The Loud Family Linen." November 13, 1885.

———. "Parson Downs Causes Another Sensation." August 2, 1886.

Worcester Daily Spy. "Boston Dispatches the Downs Scandal." February 6, 1886.

———. "The Bowdoin Square Scandal." November 7, 1885.

———. "A Sensational Assault." March 3, 1886.

12. Spirit and Flesh

Boston Daily Advertiser. "[Boston; Theatre; Sunday]." July 20, 1876.

Boston Daily Globe. "Blood and Blackmail." May 28, 1884.

———. "Dr. Blood Brought Back." January 29, 1883.

———. "Dr Blood Goes Back to Prison." June 15, 1883.

———. "Dr Blood Once More Arrested." February 3, 1883.

———. "Oxygenated Air." February 4, 1876.

———. "Physician Factories." March 26, 1881.

———. "A Wily Doctor." January 27, 1883.

Boston Journal. "Clergyman Was a Spiritualist." June 3, 1899.

———. "The Holliston Baby Farm." January 25, 1875.

———. "Holliston Baby Farm Arrest of Mrs. Mary B. Reynolds." January 25, 1875.

Boston Traveler. "H.J. Hartwell, M.D." January 25, 1866.

———. "Nitrous Oxide." January 30, 1866.

———. "Two Executions." June 5, 1873.

Chapin, Bela. *The Poets of New Hampshire*. Claremont, NH: C.H. Adams, 1883.

DeWolfe, George G.B. (spirit). "Verses Composed on the Confession and Execution of Thomas W. Piper, the Convicted Belfry Murderer." Boston, 1876?

Morgan, Rev. Henry. *Boston Inside Out!* Boston: Shawmut Publishing Company, 1883.

Morris, Dee. *Boston in the Golden Age of Spiritualism.* Charleston, SC: The History Press, 2014.
Nelson, G.K. *Spiritualism and Society.* New York: Routledge, 2014.
The New England Quarterly. "Cleansing the Puritan City." September 1, 1981.
Patriot. "Dr Blood Heard From." January 22, 1891.
Salem Register. "Amusements." May 17, 1875.
———. "Local Items." May 20, 1875.

13. The Wickedest Man in Boston

Ancestry.com. "Emery Boardman Cobb." search.ancestry.com.
The Boston Almanac and Business Directory. Boston: Sampson, Davenport, 1877.
Boston Daily Advertiser. "The Police Hearing." February 7, 1885.
Boston Daily Globe. "Captain Cain, Sir!" February 16, 1888.
———. "Fine Faro Furniture." August 12, 1885.
———. "Pomeroy's Evil Eye." August 17, 1891.
———. "'Possum' Policy Playing." February 4, 1885.
———. "Racing Rollers." May 11, 1885.
———. "Rooting Them Out." September 7, 1885.
———. "Sequel of the Great Walk." November 9, 1886.
———. "Shot by His Companion." August 7, 1885.
———. "Snowden's Lead." May 13, 1885.
The Boston Directory (1870). Boston: Sampson & Murdock Co., 1870.
The Boston Directory (1875). Boston: Sampson, Davenport, & Co., 1875.
The Boston Directory (1880). Boston, 1879.
Boston Herald. "Bose Cobb Again." September 27, 1885.
———. "Capt. Foster Put on Retired List." December 23, 1903.
———. "'Jumping Jim's' Dilemma." November 10, 1885.
———. "'Jumping Jim' Surprised." September 6, 1885.
———. "Old Time Free and Easies." August 12, 1889.
———. "One of Boston's Bad Men Gone to Settle His Account." May 12, 1889.
———. "A Perjurers' Confession." April 18, 1884.
———. "Policeman Promoted." February 16, 1888.
———. "A Saturday Night Row." April 15, 1891.
———. "Shameless Girls." September 26, 1885.
———. "War on the Gamblers." June 20, 1884.
Boston Journal. "A Successful Raid." September 7, 1885.

Boston Post. "Five Gambling Houses Raided." August 12, 1885.

———. "Jim Henderson in Court." September 18, 1885.

———. "State House Shadowed a Nest of Criminals." October 13, 1895.

Boston Sunday Globe. "A Bagnio Raided." September 6, 1885

———. "Captain Hurley's Men." September 20, 1885.

———. "Capt. Cain Drove Out Bose Cobb." August 30, 1899.

———. "Crack Skaters." May 17, 1885.

———. "Was It Accidental?" August 9, 1885.

Duis, Perry R. *The Saloon*. Chicago: University of Illinois Press, 1983.

Emerging Civil War. "Fact List About the 23rd United States Colored Troops." emergingcivilwar.com.

Lane, Roger. *Roots of Violence in Black Philadelphia, 1860–1900*. Cambridge, MA: Harvard University Press, 1989.

Seventh Annual Report of the N.E. Society for the Suppression of Vice. Boston: Deland & Barta, 1885.

14. John Bull and the Mellen Conspiracy

Boston Daily Advertiser. "Advertisement." April 6, 1878.

———. "Arrested for Receiving Stolen Property." June 1, 1870.

———. "A Merchant Arrested for Fraud." November 14, 1878.

Boston Daily Globe. "Coolidge and Cobb." October 31, 1885.

———. "The Mystery." November 2, 1885.

———. "No Escape Now." November 25, 1893.

———. "To Be Removed." October 26, 1885.

Boston Evening Transcript. "'Straw Bail.'" January 19, 1852.

Boston Herald. "Affairs About Home." September 27, 1870.

———. "Arraignment of 'John Bull.'" April 12, 1879.

———. "Big Blackmail Scheme." October 29, 1885.

———. "The Bull Case." July 22, 1879.

———. "Discovered in Mexico." January 2, 1886.

———. "Mellen at Baltimore." November 1, 1885.

———. "The M. Frank Paige Case." February 11, 1879.

———. "The Missing Mellen." November 13, 1885.

———. "Mr. Mellen Found." October 28, 1885.

———. "Mrs. Coolidge's Career." November 2, 1885.

———. "Sentenced." April 6, 1886.

Boston Journal. "Arrest of M.F. Paige." November 14, 1878.

———. "Bail Reduced." August 9, 1879.

———. "Embezzlement at City Hall." January 17, 1870.

———. "The Irregularity in the Office of the City Treasury." January 18, 1870.

———. "The John Bull Case." July 18, 1879.

———. "The John Bull Trial." July 19, 1879.

———. "Mr. Frank Paige's Failure." November 9, 1878.

———. "The Paige Straw Bail Case." February 13, 1879.

———. "[The Police Scandal; Collins; Treasury; Committee; Col.]." January 20, 1870.

———. "A Queer Story." October 27, 1885.

———. "The Recent Defalcation at City Hall the Prisoner's Statement Boston Gambling Houses Shown Up." March 15, 1870.

Boston Post. "Guilty." March 17, 1886.

———. "The John Bull Trial." July 21, 1879.

———. "The Straw Bail—The Paige Case." February 12, 1879.

Boston Traveler. "The City Treasury Defalcation." January 18, 1870.

———. "James Donahoe." September 28, 1870.

———. "Municipal Court." June 7, 1870.

———. "The Robbery of the City Treasury." January 17, 1870.

———. "Trial for Receiving Stolen Property." September 29, 1870.

Charleston News and Courier. "A Tale of Two Cities." October 28, 1885.

National Aegis. "Fighting the Tiger." March 19, 1870.

———. "The Last Defalcation." January 22, 1870.

New York Herald. "Hiring a Man to Do Murder." October 27, 1885.

———. "Sifting the 'Conspiracy.'" October 29, 1885.

New York Times. "Boston's Last Sensation." October 28, 1885.

———. "Mrs. Coolidge Pleads Guilty." March 17, 1885.

New York World. "Will Arrest Mr. Mellen." November 10, 1885.

Savage, Edward Hartwell. *Police Records and Recollections.* Boston: John P. Dale & Company, 1873.

Springfield Republican. "Eastern Massachusetts." June 1, 1870.

Trenton Evening Times. "A Plot for a Novel." October 28, 1885.

15. The End of an Era

Boston Daily Globe. "Bose Cobb's Dead." May 12, 1889.

———. "Chinese All Found Guilty." March 8, 1908.

———. "One Thing and Another." June 23, 1886.

Boston Globe. "Bose Cobb's Burial." May 14, 1889.

Boston Herald. "Bose Cobb Redivivus." February 28, 1886.

———. "Bose Cobb's Place Closed." January 2, 1886.

———. "Death of 'Bose' Cobb." May 12, 1889.

———. "The North Street Homicide—Inquest on the Body of Ford." November 25, 1862.

———. "Old Time Free and Easies." August 12, 1889.

———. "One of Boston's Bad Men Gone to Settle His Account." May 12, 1889.

———. "Policeman Promoted." February 16, 1888.

Boston Journal. "A Cripple for Life." January 18, 1901.

Boston Post. "Dead Man Found on Car Top." January 18, 1901.

———. "Murderous Affray in North St." November 24, 1862.

Boston Sunday Post. "Warry S. Charles Arrested as Accessory to Chinese Murders." August 11, 1907.

Boston Traveler. "Murder in North Street—The Notorious Barney Ford Killed." November 25, 1862.

Brighton Allston Historical Society. "Allston-Brighton Tornado of 1888." www.bahistory.org.

Elkhart Daily Review. "Boston Loses a Very Wicked Man." May 14, 1889.

Evening Star. "Sequel of the Downs Scandal." August 16, 1886.

Historic Camera. "Elmer Chickering." historiccamera.com.

Klein, Christopher. *Strong Boy*. Guilford, CT: Lyons Press, 2013.

Kruh, David. *Always Something Doing*. Boston: Faber and Faber, 1990.

Miller, Neil. *Banned in Boston*. Boston: Beacon Press, 2010.

New Haven Register. "Not So Bad after All." June 3, 1889.

New York Times. "Butler for Pastor Downs." December 21, 1886.

———. "Warry S. Charles Arrested." August 11, 1907.

O'Neill, Gerard. *Rogues and Redeemers*. New York: Crown Publishers, 2012.

Steen, Ivan D. "Cleansing the Puritan City: The Reverend Henry Morgan's Antivice Crusade in Boston." *New England Quarterly* (September 1981).

ABOUT THE AUTHOR

*R*obert Wilhelm is the author of *Murder and Mayhem in Essex County* (The History Press), a history of capital crimes in Essex County, Massachusetts, from the 1600s to the turn of the twentieth century; and *The Bloody Century* (Night Stick Press), a compilation of true tales of murder in nineteenth-century America. He blogs about historical true crime at Murder by Gaslight (www.murderbygaslight.com) and the National Night Stick (www.night-stick.com). Robert lives a fine, upstanding life in the city of Boston, Massachusetts.

www.ingramcontent.com/pod-product-compliance
Lightning Source LLC
Chambersburg PA
CBHW070949200526
45161CB00001BA/44